COMMUNICATION SERIES

How to Find Your Way Around the Internet

Written by Kathryn Toyer
Edited by National Press Publications

NATIONAL PRESS PUBLICATIONS
A Division of Rockhurst College Continuing Education Center, Inc.
6901 West 63rd Street • P.O. Box 2949 • Shawnee Mission, Kansas 66201-1349
1-800-258-7248 • 1-913-432-7757

National Press Publications endorses nonsexist language. In an effort to make this handbook clear, consistent and easy to read, we've used "he" throughout the odd-numbered chapters and "she" throughout the even-numbered chapters. The copy is not intended to be sexist.

How to Find Your Way Around the Internet
Published by National Press Publications, Inc.

A Division of Rockhurst College Continuing Education Center, Inc.

Printed in the United States of America

1 2 3 4 5 6 7 8 9 10

ISBN 1-55852-206-9

HOW TO FIND YOUR WAY AROUND THE INTERNET

Table of Contents

Introduction 1

1 Learning from Your Visitors/Customers 5

2 Communicate with Newsgroups 15

3 Keep in Touch with E-Mail 29

4 Talk with IRC — Internet Relay Chat 45

5 Search the Libraries with Gopher 57

6 Get Those Files with FTP — File Transfer Protocol 67

7 Search Networks and Databases with WAIS 75

8 Get to Places with Telnet 83

9 Interact with Customers Using the World Wide Web 91

10 Conclusion 107

Index of Internet Sites 111

General Index 122

INTRODUCTION

The Internet was originally designed for the military. They wanted a communications tool that would remain working even if a part of it was destroyed or disabled. With the advent of a universal computer language, the Internet was born in 1969. Universities, researchers and scientists began using this massive network of computers to share information and research. As more information was made available, tools were designed to assist users in finding and exchanging that information. With the development of all these new tools it became easier to access and provide information, so more information was poured into the Internet. For more than 20 years the Internet amassed volumes of usable information, but it was only accessible by the military, universities, researchers and scientists.

With the help of the Information Act of 1992, the Internet became accessible to the general public, which increased the amount of information being distributed significantly, and since 1993 the Internet has experienced a population explosion. In fact, the number of users increased more in the past two years than in the whole history of the Internet combined. The amount of information grows daily and with every new person who gets connected.

The Internet offers you a vast resource of information. You can find almost anything you want to know about your customers, your competition, the financial marketplace and vendors. It contains information about your competition like business reports and catalogs. You can now quickly assess how both competitors and friends are presenting themselves to the public.

One of the major goals you have as a business is customer satisfaction. You spend thousands of dollars to find out what your customers are doing and how they feel about you. The Internet will let you find out what your customers are doing at a fraction of your current expenditure. Many of your existing customers are already online, many of them will be coming online soon and many potential customers are out there waiting for you.

Whether you're a small business wanting to grow or a larger business wanting to stay on the fast track, the Internet can save you time and put a wealth of valuable knowledge at your fingertips or mouse click. The Internet by its very nature is the best and quickest way for you to research information. Learn to use it to get customers to tell you what you need to know.

If you've taken a look around the Internet, one of the things that probably struck you right from the start is that there's a lot of information out there. You probably felt overwhelmed by the sheer volume. You may even have felt that, because there's so much information on the Internet and you have so little knowledge and training using this research tool, that it's futile to even try. You may have even tried to find a few things and found yourself chasing down blind alleys with little more information than what you started with.

Not only is there an overabundance of information out there, but it's not organized in any logical order. As a matter of fact, it's not organized at all. Each service on the Internet contains its own type of information and its own way of storing it. Some of the information you need is contained on only one of these services. Some of it may even be duplicated or be included in part or in whole in one or more of the other services. If you are new to the Internet, it's often frustrating and discouraging trying to find just the right piece of information you need. If only you knew the right place to begin your search, half your job would be done. Most of your frustration would be alleviated. In this book we are going to talk about the various kinds of information available on the Internet, how to access it and how to use the tools of the Internet. We will also show you how to conduct research on the Internet.

If in the "real world" if you want to get information about your customers, you would use one of two means: you would ask them questions to get them to tell you directly what you need to know, or, you would use other means to get that information from them. You might sponsor in-store promotions, sweepstakes or giveaways. Then your marketing department would tally the number of visitors you had against your sales. They might even compare the number of new customers generated by that promotion against the number of repeat customers. We will teach you how to use these same techniques and which Internet services they should be used with to get the best results.

You'll also learn where to go to look for and find product information and how to find out what others in your industry are doing. You'll learn how to find research that has been done on a product you're considering offering to your customers. We'll show you how to search for and locate software or utilities to enhance or upgrade your current system. No matter what kind of research you need to do, with the millions of files and documents on the Internet, chances are good you can find it there. We'll teach which service holds what information and where to start your search. We'll teach you how to use that service to your advantage, to get to the information you need quickly.

For some of you, especially those just getting started, the Internet is a maze of computer babble and confusing resources. For others, it's a little more clearly defined in your mind, but you still haven't found much of value. Still others of you are ready to do heavy duty research and just need a place to start. This book will address each of your needs.

Determining where to start your search, whether you're a beginner or an expert, is often the most difficult task. Know which one of the Internet services is best for finding the information you need can be a research headache in itself.

In this book we've broken down each of the Internet services by what information they contain and how you can use them. We've separated them into two categories for you. The first category includes the services you would use to gather information directly from your customers — the communication tools. The second category contains the services that let you get information indirectly from your customer or files of information you would need to complete research into your product, industry, government policies or legislation, etc.

In the first category you have the communication tools of newsgroups, e-mail and IRC — Internet Relay Chat. You'll learn how to use each of these tools to communicate directly with customers. We'll teach you to use each of these to locate and talk to experts, vendors, or potential employees. You'll learn how to use these tools to make your business grow and keep your customers satisfied.

The second category contains the indirect and research tools of FTP — File Transfer Protocol, Gopher, WAIS, Telnet and the World Wide Web. You'll learn what kind of information each of these tools contain, such as: scientific research, libraries, bulletin board systems, software, databases, etc. We'll also teach you how to use each of these tools to find the particular kind of information you need. You'll learn how to use the World Wide Web indirectly to get your customers to give you information, how to use FTP to locate catalogs and software, how to use Gopher to keep up with current legislation that could affect your business, how to use WAIS to search indexed databases — both your own and those on the Internet — and how to use Telnet to access libraries and bulletin board systems to keep up with industry trends.

Used effectively, as we'll teach you in this book, each of these tools can provide you with a wealth of information about your customers, help you get more customers and find out what your competition is doing. You'll learn to use these tools to keep up with laws that could impact your business and to stay abreast of industry or financial trends. The Internet and its services can help you build your business, make it stronger and let you provide better customer service.

Everything you do with conventional research can now be done in less time, in the comfort of your home or office and at a fraction of the cost. When you complete this book you will have a good understanding of the Internet tools and a solid strategy for finding what you want from the Internet.

1 LEARNING FROM YOUR VISITORS/CUSTOMERS

As a business person you are interested in finding out what your customers want, think and feel. Your business depends on it and you spend thousands of dollars for just that purpose. You hire telemarketing teams, market researchers and send out tons of mail a year to get information from and about your customers.

You spend thousands of dollars each year sending your customers surveys and conducting customer satisfaction polls. When you design these surveys and polls, you phrase your questions to ensure that your customers give you the information you need to improve your product or service. You even ask them questions that will tell you how you can sell to them.

You hire market research teams or firms to conduct this research for you. You give them the responsibility of tallying the results of your surveys and polls and report back to you. They tell you what their findings are and what you need to do.

You also hire customer service representatives to talk to your customers. Their job is to listen to what the customers are saying and report to you. You use this information to locate your weak areas and implement policies to improve your business.

The Internet gives you an additional means to get that same information from your customers. It can also allow you to do this at a substantial savings to you, both in time and money. It also allows you to reach a broader base of customers. It allows you to be open around the clock — to be there for your customers when they need you.

There are two ways you can get information from your customers — directly or indirectly. Using direct methods like e-mail, newsgroups and IRC, you can go straight to your customers. You can interact with them quickly and easily for a fraction of the traditional costs. You can go directly to your customer with an e-mail, post an opinion survey in a newsgroup, or conduct a live focus group on IRC. You are going to communicate directly and interact with your customers electronically.

By using indirect methods like the World Wide Web, you can also get information about your customers. You can use tracking software to find out where they go when they visit your site, find out where they lingered, and, you can even use it to find out which of your products are hot and which are cold. You can use games, giveaways and sweepstakes to attract customers to you, then track where they go and what they do while they're there. With indirect methods you're going to use programs or tools to let your customers give you information about themselves.

You'll use the other tools of FTP, Gopher, WAIS and Telnet to help you locate information to make better business decisions, improve or protect your business and keep on the fast track. You will use FTP to locate software and utilities to upgrade or enhance your computer system, locate the sales catalogs or product updates of your competition, or provide information for your customers to download to their systems. Gopher will help you to keep up with labor statistics and climate and cultural information about areas around the world, legal issues and legislation that could impact your business and training materials to keep your employees ahead of the game. Telnet and WAIS will let you search libraries and archives for bibliographies and research on your industry to keep you current with what your industry is doing.

DIRECT METHODS

In many ways business is the same today as it's always been. For example, you know that to be productive and professional in business you must talk to your customers. And, whether you stand at the door greeting them, conduct surveys or send an e-mail, you must talk to your customers and listen to what they have to say!

LEARNING FROM YOUR VISITORS/CUSTOMERS

One of the best ways to get information from your customers is to question them directly. Customer surveys and satisfaction polls allow them to tell you what you can do to improve your product or service. In traditional marketing you probably have the surveys designed, printed and mailed out. Then you sit back and wait for your customers to respond to your survey. Sometimes you wait weeks, maybe even months for a return of generally less than 25%. Even after waiting all that time, the results you get back are sometimes disappointing, at best. As inefficient as it is, this direct approach helps you gather information from your customers.

Today you can take those very same customer surveys using the Internet. According to a recent survey, e-mail is 83% more likely to get a response!

When you get a survey in the mail, what do you do with it? If you're like most people, you go through your mail, sort it according to importance and trash the junk. Most of our mail today goes in the trash. But are surveys junk mail? Sometimes they are. With a traditional mail response survey, you must open, read, fill out and remail the survey. Separate steps that take time and commitment.

Time is something most of us don't have much of these days. Many of us set aside time during the weekends to go through our mail again. We come across a survey, look it over, fill it out and post it — assuming we have a pencil handy, an envelope and label, a stamp and a convenient mailbox. But, maybe you, like many people, decide you just can't be bothered and toss it in the trash. Is it any wonder why so few are returned?

When you send that same survey out over the Internet, you get a different response. You get more responses and you get them quicker. Let's look at the same survey as it hits the Internet. First, the customer doesn't stack, sort, or tote any paper. It's point and click. Being organized or misplacing e-mail is just not a significant problem. Whenever your customer is ready to read your e-mail survey, it's a mouse click away. Second, there is no need to look for a pencil, envelope or stamp. Your customer simply uses their key responder and it's on its way!

The second reason e-mail generates such a positive response is the very nature of the Internet. The culture and climate of the Internet is benevolent, cooperative and spontaneous. It was designed to be a resource for positive interaction from the very beginning and that tone survives today. As the Internet evolves, we may become hardened to e-mail as we are to junk mail and even the telephone. But for today, e-mail works!

There are several companies on the Internet that will design surveys, maintain your customer information and tabulate the results for you. One such company is Data Star, Inc. You can find the address for this company in the section at the back of this book called Index of Internet Sites.

A well-constructed online survey (see insert) allows your customer to simply click and complete your survey. Data Star, Inc. states that electronic surveys allow the respondent to jump around to the areas that pertain to them, therefore limiting the time it takes for them to complete them.

Filling out a survey online can be as fun and easy as playing a computer game. Respondents use their mouse to click on the little boxes beside the selections that are true. Then they click on the send button and off it goes, into cyberland and back to your e-mail box.

Information gathering isn't new to businesses. The Internet, however, has made competitive analysis cost effective. The expense for conducting this customer-responsive research is traditionally quite costly. It can run as high as $120 per hour, limiting this kind of research to the larger corporations.

The Internet gives you a medium to conduct this same research without the high cost, although you are still going to have some of the same costs of traditional research. You're still going to have a person or persons dedicated to conducting the research you need. Some of the databases you will want to research charge an hourly fee; however, that fee is substantially less than what you pay an outside resource — $24 per hour versus $120 per hour. Using the Internet, you will save on postage and data entry. You will get more for your money using the Internet because it gives you more timely information. You'll be getting it at the speed of light from

Questions can be short open-ends...

1. What is your job title or primary job function:

2. What Web Browser do you use:

Responses can be pre-listed, in either a single-response fashion...

3. When was the first time you "connected to" or "browsed" the World-Wide-Web?

- This is my first time
- Within the last 6 months
- Within the last year
- More than 1 year ago

...or allow for multiple responses...

4. What prompted you to visit our Web site? *(please check all that apply)*

- Received postcard or other mailing from DataStar
- Someone at DataStar told me about it
- Referral from a friend or business associate
- Through an Internet search engine
- A link from some other site (please specify:)
- Some other source (please specify:)

Rating questions....

5. What is your overall opinion of our Web Site and Sample Survey? *(Select anywhere on the below scale with your mouse...)*

"Not impressed" ● ● ● ● ● ● ● ● ● ● "Really cool!"

Pull down menu question....

6. What state are you visiting from? *(Click the arrow with your mouse to view your options...)* STATE

Responses to open-ended questions can be entered directly...

7. What could we do to improve or enhance our Web site?

your customers. You'll be getting it as soon as it's made available, whether that be to a newsgroup, a mailing list, or a database. You can still hire someone on the outside to do your research for you. Many of them even advertise on the World Wide Web. The beauty of the Internet is that you don't have to contract it out, you can do it yourself!

When you use the Internet to conduct your research you will be able to get the same, if not better results at a fraction of the cost of conventional market researching. You won't have paper costs, the cost of postage, the cost of faxes or long distance phone calls. You cut out the distribution costs. You can communicate with people anywhere in the world for the cost of a local phone call. You can even find employees with this powerful communication tool.

INDIRECT METHODS

The Internet not only allows you direct access to customers — it also has a wide range of tools that you can use to provide information to your customers. You can gather an extraordinary amount of good customer information, indirectly, by learning how to use the Internet tools as a business resource. We've just explored how you can conduct your market research using direct communication methods. Next, we'll discuss indirect methods of gathering information.

You pay a bundle to attract more customer traffic to your business. Your business is measured in how many people purchase products or services from you. You probably even host promotions and sales to attract more people. Then you record the success of your advertising against added customer sales.

What is it worth to you, or your business, to know what really worked in your ad campaign? Do you know for sure how much business your advertising really generated last year? Even the best campaigns can only "ball park" an answer. But with the Internet, you can tell how long a customer looked at a picture, if they skipped past certain details, and, you can tell with a high degree of certainty what really interests your customer.

Imagine catalogs that can quickly be modified to eliminate low response products. Imagine what it would be like to know for sure what your customer touched and lingered around. And imagine that they can't shop-lift any of it!

The methods you use currently can be expanded to the Internet. You can track the number of visitors you have. You can sponsor contests. You can even offer premiums for visiting your business. The Internet, and the World Wide Web in particular, gives you the opportunity to create a store front accessible to the whole world, and, using the tools of the Internet, marketing can indirectly access trends and tendencies.

The World Wide Web comes equipped with graphics, text, sound and video to create multimedia pages of information. These tools allow you to create pages of information about your business, product or service, much as you would for sales brochures, catalogs or magazine advertisements — but at a fraction of the cost.

LEARNING FROM YOUR VISITORS/CUSTOMERS

The World Wide Web has millions of Web pages, and that number increases daily. As the public and businesses have gained access to the Internet the World Wide Web has grown exponentially. Today, it's where businesses go to advertise their products and exchange services.

Because it's where businesses go to advertise, businesses wanted a way to find out how many people were visiting their Web sites each day. Software was developed that tracks the number of times a Web site has been visited. In Internet jargon, these are called "hits."

You can set this software to tell you where your customers travel within your Web site, where they lingered and what interests them. You can use it with your sales catalog to tell you which products are hot — which ones attracted the most interest. Use it to tell you which products are cold — the ones that were skipped over.

Once you decide to create a place for people to visit and a way to track them, how do you get them there and keep them there? One way to do this is to offer games or giveaways in your Web site. When you include games and giveaways in your Web site, you not only attract visitors and entice them to stay — you gain valuable information about them.

Here is what you can do to gather information about your customers. You can include a short questionnaire for the visitors to fill out before or after they play your game or get your gift. If you include a game in your Web site, you will want to keep it simple and quick.

You'll want to include a game your customers can play in a few minutes, and that is somehow connected to your business. The giveaway may be something they can download from your site, such as a screen saver. Or it could be something they have to request from you, which would require them to give you information.

Whether you use games or giveaways, you can include a short questionnaire for them to fill out. You will want to allow them to give you information about themselves such as their name, address, phone number, e-mail address, etc. You could also include a few questions about how they found you, or what product or service of yours they use. Be careful not to turn this into a customer survey. You don't want to take up too much of their time here. You can include a survey in a different area of your Web site, as mentioned above.

CBS, the television network, uses their Web site to get as much information from their customers as they can. You'll notice in **http:/ www.clos.com**, a view of their home page, that they have included a customer survey or poll, a contest and a giveaway. They have also included their e-mail address and a request that visitors send them their comments or questions.

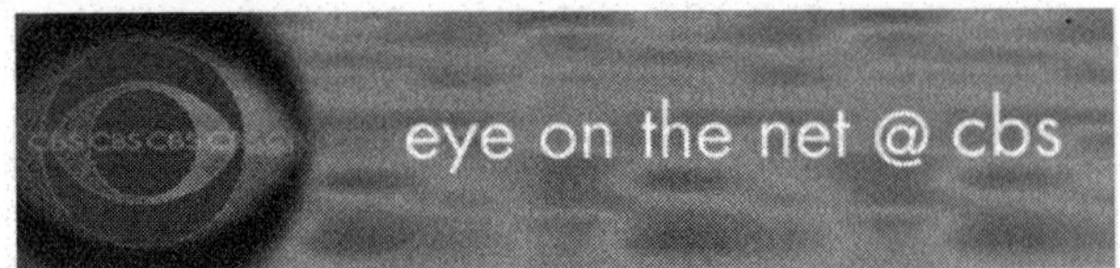

Hi, Today is Wednesday, February 28, 1996

- Check out the LATE SHOW WITH DAVID LETTERMAN. Tonight's guests include actor Susan Sarandon, actor/comedian Rob Schneider and singer Ray Davies.
- Watch THE 38th ANNUAL GRAMMY AWARDS live tonight at 8:00 PM/ET. Do you want the chance to WIN A TRIP TO A MYSTERY CONCERT? Take a look!
- Don't miss our CBS Sports College Basketball site where you can play Hoop Picks, for your chance to **WIN** exciting prizes, and cast your **VOTE** in the College Basketball Fan Poll.
- Find out the winner of the PILLSBURY BAKE-OFF and get the $1,000,000 recipe.

DOWNLOAD **the New CBS Eye Screensaver.**

LATE SHOW with David Letterman* | *The Late Late Show with Tom Snyder
CBS Daytime* | *CBS Sports* | *Eyeware Gallery* | *You're On* | *Remotes
CBS News Up To The Minute* | *Black Rock* | *Dr. Quinn Medicine Woman
Touched By An Angel

Check out the CBS *F.A.Q. LIST* for answers to your frequently asked questions.

We want to hear from you, so please send your comments and questions via our comments form or by e-mail to marketing@cbs.com.

Special Note: One thing you must remember about Web pages is that in order for businesses to keep visitors coming back they must constantly update their Web pages. Many change them weekly or monthly. *CBS* updates theirs on a daily basis. So, when you view their site, it will probably not look the same as shown here.

SUMMARY

You need information to conduct your business and improve your products or services. You need information about your customers, your competition, market trends and financial issues. You can get this information either through direct or indirect means. Using the Internet you can communicate directly with your customers by using e-mail, newsgroups or IRC, Internet Relay Chat. Indirectly you can get information from them by using tracking software, games, or giveaways.

By using surveys you can get information directly from your customers and visitors. By communicating directly with your customers using either newsgroups, e-mail, or IRC, you can interact with your customers and get them to tell you directly how they think and feel. Indirectly you can track the number of visitors to your Web site and entice them to stay and give you more information by including games and giveaways in your Web site. The Internet gives you the tools to interact with your customers and visitors, or to gather information from them. Internet gives you information faster and at a lower cost to you.

LEARNING FROM YOUR VISITORS/CUSTOMERS

1. The Internet gives you an additional means to get information from your customers.
   a. true
   b. false

2. There are two ways you can get information from your customers:
   a. the World Wide Web and WAIS
   b. FTP and Gopher
   c. directly and indirectly

3. When you send a survey out over the Internet:
   a. the customer has to be organized in order to fill it out
   b. you get more responses and quicker
   c. you make it harder for them to fill it out and return to you

4. Putting catalogs online:
   a. would be of no benefit to your business
   b. leaves you no way to eliminate low response products
   c. lets you know what products your customer's touched and lingered around

5. The World Wide Web will:
   a. only let you do research
   b. create Web pages of information about your business
   c. is a text-only medium

ANSWER KEY: 1. a, 2. c, 3. b, 4. c, 5. b

2 COMMUNICATE WITH NEWSGROUPS

WHAT NEWSGROUPS ARE

Usenet newsgroups, or newsgroups for short, began in the early '80s as a means for researchers to post articles or news of their findings. As articles were posted, other researchers posted their comments or questions regarding the article. That same forum of findings, comments and questions still exists today. In addition, newsgroups evolved into discussion groups where people with similar interests exchanged ideas and information. There are literally thousands of topics being discussed on these newsgroups. Topics range from antiques to zoology, computers to money market funds.

Newsgroups is one of the direct methods you'll use to gather information. It's one of the communication tools of the Internet. You'll use it to communicate directly with customers, vendors, potential employees and experts in their fields.

You'll find newsgroups that contain target market groups such as: rec.running, where they exchange questions and answers and tips; alt.mothers, where they exchange advice and tips on mothering; misc.rural, where they give support and tips on living in rural America; or even soc.genealogy, where they exchange stories and tips on charting their family trees. Use these to conduct market research.

In every newsgroup, you will find experts that can help you improve your product or service. Use them to help you with financial, marketing or system improvements. You can find them in groups like misc.invest.futures, misc.entrepeneurs or alt.aldus.pagemaker.

You can use newsgroups to help you find vendors, to talk to customers. Or, use them to find out what your customers are thinking, how they feel about your product or service, how they feel about your competition.

The first thing to understand about the Usenet is that it's big, very big. Usenet newsgroups began in universities and many sites reside in them, including research labs or other academic institutions. When the Internet opened up to the public these Usenet sites evolved into commercial entities. Commercial newsgroup sites now outnumber the academic sites.

However, no one group or person has authority over the Usenet. There is no Usenet Incorporated. Because of this you will find newsgroups covering almost every topic conceivable.

HOW NEWSGROUPS WORK

Your Internet provider will offer many Usenet newsgroups. Most newsgroups are offered at no charge to you, but there are some that do charge a fee. Usually the fee is not a large one, and some of the best information is only a few cents away.

There are literally thousands of topics available to you. Most providers will not offer all of the newsgroups that are available. This is largely due to management and space issues. However, you will find that they are willing to provide newsgroups that are of interest to their subscribers. The first place to start is to identify what is available to you.

Each newsgroup on the Usenet contains what are called "posts" from the members of the group. These posts are messages that contain questions, discussions of the topic, comments or advice from the participants. You may at any time choose to read just the posts to each group. As you explore what's available to you, you will find groups you'll want to join. This is called "subscribing." When you subscribe to a group you become a member of that group. You can then begin posting your own messages and participate in the discussions. Being part of the group, you can now reply to other members' posts, send e-mail to the group, or, to an individual from the group.

COMMUNICATE WITH NEWSGROUPS

How would you like the expert opinions of the world's best minds on TQM (Total Quality Management)? Or maybe you're considering installing a new voice-activated mail system and would like to know how it really works. Would you like instant access to ideas and opinions on the marketplace? Do you ever wonder if there's a place to bounce ideas around before you take the leap? Well, that's what Usenet newsgroups are designed to offer. You can find an abundance of information on the various newsgroups that can help to make you a better decision maker.

When you connect to the Usenet, you will have several options available to you. You can read, subscribe, post, reply and send e-mail to any newsgroups or to the individual people participating in the discussions.

The major newsgroups fall into one of the following categories:

* Miscellaneous — .misc — contain categories of newsgroups that don't fit anywhere else. This is where you'll find groups like misc.consumers, misc.business.consulting, misc.business.credit, misc.business.records-mgmt, misc.taxes, or misc.invest.stocks. These are the groups you will want to research to find your target markets. Some of them will also contain those experts you're looking for.

* Recreational — .rec — will contain many of your target market groups. These groups cover topics about hobbies and sports like rec.crafts, rec.boats, rec.hunting, or rec.skiing. This group and the miscellaneous group are where you might concentrate your market research, and where you'll find specific demographic groups.

* Social — .soc — discussion of various social issues in groups like soc.religion, soc.support, soc.genealogy, or soc.culture. This is the category you will research to keep up to date on international social issues and histories. You'll be able to locate experts to help you make decisions about how and where to market.

* Science — .sci — are where you are going to find scientific experts. You'll find them in groups like sci.electronics, sci.med, sci.engr, or sci.energy. You'll use these experts to answer your technical questions or to help you research areas where you may be lacking technical expertise within your company.

* News — .news — contain the experts and the information you need to create your own newsgroup. You'll find them in groups like news.announce.newsgroups, news.misc, or news.groups.

* Computer — .comp — are where you're going to find computer experts. You'll want to send your Management Information System (MIS) person or yourself to these groups to keep up to date or to get help with those sticky computer problems. You'll find lots of information and an abundance of help on groups like comp.databases, comp.home.automation, comp.networks or comp.security.

* Alternative — .alt — discuss topics that are outside the ordinary, or that are strange or weird. You may have heard the stories on the national and local news broadcasts about sex on the Internet. This is one of the categories where sex is being discussed. If you have children this is one of the areas of the Internet you may wish to monitor. However, there are also groups here that could be of value to you. You can find groups like alt.genealogy, alt.smokers, alt.left-handed, alt.real-estate-agents, alt.mothers, alt.new-england, or alt.architecture. You'll be able to find some of your target markets and some experts in these groups.

* Business — .biz — are the semi-commercial set of commercial groups. You'll find groups like biz.books.technical, biz.comp, biz.general, biz.comp.accounting, or biz.marketplace. These are the groups you can search to find out about your competition or other vendors. You'll also look here for experts in your industry. The .biz newsgroups tend to be very sensitive to business concerns, and you'll probably find many kindred souls here.

Each newsgroup will have category designation followed by the topic. Some examples are shown below.

untitled

33 groups

1052	alt.business.import-export
79	alt.business.import-export.computer
67	alt.business.import-export.raw-material
57	alt.business.insurance
54	alt.business.internal-audit
57	alt.business.offshore
160	alt.business.seminars
3	alt.culture.french-polynesia
67	alt.culture.indonesia
143	alt.culture.internet
22	alt.culture.military-brats
245	alt.current-events.bosnia
285	alt.current-events.usa
406	alt.drugs.psychedelics
6	alt.education.university.vision2020
106	alt.games.vampire.the.masquerade
161	alt.games.wing-commander
13	alt.health.oxygen-therapy
10	alt.music.underworld
71	bit.listserv.basque-l
15	bit.listserv.c370-l
484	bit.listserv.catala
1	comp.database
5	comp.database.oracle
143	comp.databases.ms-sqlserver
47	comp.dcom.net-management
138	comp.lang.basic.visual.3rdparty
3	misc.education.multimedia
365	misc.entrepreneurs.moderated
64	misc.industry.electronics.marketplace
1754	rec.autos.sport.indy
4595	rec.autos.sport.nascar
501	rec.outdoors.fishing.fly

Full Group List

15932 groups

sci.engr.chem
sci.engr.civil
sci.engr.color
sci.engr.control
sci.engr.geomechanics
sci.engr.heat-vent-ac
sci.engr.lighting
sci.engr.manufacturing
sci.engr.marine
sci.engr.marine.hydrodynamics
sci.engr.mech
sci.engr.metallurgy
sci.engr.safety
sci.engr.semiconductors
sci.engr.surveying
sci.engr.television
sci.engr.television.advanced
sci.engr.television.broadcast
sci.environment
sci.fractals
sci.geo
sci.geo.earthquakes
sci.geo.eos
sci.geo.fluids
sci.geo.geology
sci.geo.hydrology
sci.geo.meteorology
sci.geo.oceanography
sci.geo.petroleum
sci.geo.rivers+lakes
sci.geo.satellite-nav
sci.image
sci.image.processing

As you read through the list of categories, you probably thought, "I won't need this one or that one." Don't eliminate a category just because of its name, or because you think it's not specifically focused on your business need. Many groups have very deep roots which extend in many directions.

When you look at this partial list of groups with each of the categories, remember we told you that there were thousands of newsgroups available. You're probably wondering how you'll ever find the groups you need. You're not the first one that's faced that problem. Search tools have been designed to help you identify the newsgroup you're looking for. There are search tools that will search newsgroups by keyword and produce a report for you, listing newsgroups that match your keyword.

DejaNews is one of the best search tools for locating the newsgroups you need. You can find them at: **http://www.dejanews.com**. InfoSeek is another search tool you can use to help you locate just the right newsgroup. You can find them at: **http://www.inforseek.com**. Another search tool that will search newsgroups is Alta Vista, located at: **http://www.altavista.digital.com**. Others will be listed in the Index of Internet Sites section in the back of this book. These search tools save you time, and they can help you find the newsgroups that will be best for your business needs.

Once you find your group or groups, follow the posts or threads (series of posts), for a while. Get familiar with the group and the discussion. If you're looking for quality information, but you're having trouble sifting though the pile of information, look for people who frequently post. These people will either be nuts or very credible! Simply follow the path of greatest frequency. If they have time to post, they'll probably answer an e-mail inquiry from you. Also, look for certain addresses like Microsoft, Netcom, or others from major companies. Many of them have a full-time staff to provide quality information in these newsgroups.

Look for common themes or questions. If more than one person is asking for advice or help, it's a safe bet there's a customer need you may be able to fill. You will also want to look for the FAQs. FAQs include the policies and procedures for each group. FAQ stands for Frequently Asked Questions. These FAQs will answer a lot of *your* questions about the group, such as why it was formed, what its purpose is, what is acceptable and what won't be tolerated.

While you're in a newsgroup, look at the end of each post. An interesting feature of newsgroup that you will notice as you are reading posts is something called signatures. These appear at the end of a post and are a way to show individuality or tell the group who they belong to. Many signatures include the person's e-mail address and/or Web site address. This is an area you can use to advertise your business. The signature area is similar to the way you use your letterhead on your stationary. You can include your business name, address, phone and fax number, your e-mail and your Web site address. When you're looking for experts, notice the signature file also. This will help tell you if the person is credible.

A QUICK LESSON ON NEWSGROUPS

In order to use newsgroups to find experts, conduct your market research, or get the information, you need to know how to function in, and use, the software. If you don't already have the software, you can download it at one of the two software sites listed in the Index of Internet Sites section of this book. The following lesson steps will help you fit right in:

Step One: Load the Groups. Select New Groups from the menu options and double click to load them. Then, read the posts by clicking on the ones you wish to read.

Step Two: Join Groups. To subscribe to a group, highlight it and click on the subscribe button in the tool bar, or choose subscribe from the menu options.

Step Three: Post a Message. Simply click on the post, reply, or send button in the tool bar, or select one of these options from the menu. Then compose your message and press send. If you're sending a message to an expert or an individual, you'll want to "make it private." To do this you will select "send" mail rather than post or reply.

Step Four: Keeping an Article. If you find an article you want to keep, you can keep it from being purged by clicking on the Keep the Article button in the tool bar.

Step Five: Creating a Signature. Select Signatures from the menu icons, type in your information and then select the ones you want for it.

Step Six: Compose with Thought. Think before you post.

Step Seven: Refresh newsgroups. Each day you visit the groups you will need to refresh them, to bring in the new posts. You'll do this by clicking on the Refresh Groups button in the tool bar.

COMMUNICATE WITH NEWSGROUPS

1. You'll use newsgroups to:
   a. gather information
   b. locate target groups
   c. communicate with customers
   d. all of the above

2. Your Internet provider will:
   a. offer you many newsgroups
   b. charge you for all newsgroups
   c. won't get a group for you that you're interested in

3. Each newsgroup contains posts.
   a. you have to read every post
   b. you can post your own message to them
   c. you can't send messages to individual members on the newsgroups

4. When you sign on to the Usenet, you can:
   a. subscribe to newsgroups
   b. post, reply or send to any newsgroup or individual people in the discussions
   c. both of the above

5. There is no place you can go to find the policies and procedures for each newsgroup.
   a. true
   b. false

ANSWER KEY: 1. d, 2. a, 3. b, 4. c, 5. b

HOW YOU CAN USE NEWSGROUPS FOR RESEARCH

The thousands of newsgroups that are out there offer a vast resource of information at your fingertips. You can sit back and just observe, called "lurking" on the Internet, or you can interact with the community. Lurking is not necessarily a bad thing on the Internet. If you are a new person to the internet, you are called a "newbie" and you are expected to lurk before you post, learning the ins and outs of acceptable postings. Lurking can also give you the opportunity to find out who the "experts" are on each newsgroup and find out which groups have the kind of people in them you're looking for. Lurk to learn!

As you lurk you will notice posters using abbreviations and ascii art symbols in their messages. Keep in mind that because this is a written form of communication, it is easy to offend, or come across as angry or antagonistic. When this happens it's considered a "flame." Many a "flame war" has been started by misconstrued messages. You can prevent some of this from happening or allay its effect by using some of these Internet symbols in your messages. Remember there are real people behind those keyboards and computers.

Lurking will also help you find the newsgroups that have people in your target market, vendors, potential employees or experts in the financial marketplace, marketing, or other areas to improve your business. It can help you find the groups that have information about new products, your industry or your competition. At some point you may even want to create your own newsgroup to interact with test groups, or for target market groups.

Because there are thousands of newsgroups, you will be able to find target group information in one or more of these groups. You or your market research people can join and observe the various groups until you find the group that suits your needs, or you can do a search by keyword of all the groups.

Often the best way to find your target group is to simply join a newsgroup and observe the threads, posts, and replies to those posts for a time. This will give you a feel for the environment and personalities of the participants. It will also give you a more accurate concept of the topic that's being discussed as well as the "experts" — those who really know what they're talking about — in the group(s).

At any time you feel that you can answer a question or join in the discussion, do so. If you want to link the newsgroup to your business, include an example of how you or your business would have handled a related problem in your response or answer to the question or discussion. For instance: "We had the same problem at our company, *ABC Repairs.* This is how we handled it ..." This will let the audience know that you are a business person and what kind of business you're in. As you become part of the group, you will begin getting inquiries about your product or service. As rapport is built and relationships grow, there is no limit to what you will receive.

If you need a particular product or supply, the newsgroups may be a resource for you to find vendors. For example, a woman who made wreaths out of cork decided to turn her hobby into a business — but she needed a supplier of cork. She had an Internet connection and had been wandcring around the newsgroups for some time. She subscribed to a few of the wine and wine making groups. She posted to these groups telling them what she was doing and that she needed a supplier of cork. A winery in California responded. Now she has a supplier for one of the major ingredients she needs to make her business a success. She also got to talk to a lot of people who throw away their corks. You can do this too!

If you need information about the financial marketplace, or just want to keep up to date on financial news, newsgroups can provide you with information like misc.invest.funds, misc.business.credit, or misc.invest.real-estate. Many of the people involved in these groups are part of the financial community as bankers or brokers. Your potential for finding an expert in the field is very high.

Potential employees abound on the Internet. Newsgroups afford you the opportunity to find out a little more about a person before the interview than is possible in the "real world." For instance, by joining newsgroups and observing, you can find out a lot about the individuals posting to those groups. You can find out their areas of expertise, their personalities, their writing style, professionalism, the way they approach issues and how they handle problems, simply by observing. When you find someone you feel would be a good candidate for you, send them an e-mail or offer them the opportunity to talk, interview, and even join your company.

Just as you are joining the newsgroups for research and information gathering, so is your competition. And, if they're not out there, chances are good that someone in these groups is talking about them or their product. Search until you find what you're looking for, or you can start up a discussion with carefully phrased posts to get the group talking about your competition. You can direct the conversation by posting a question or posing a topic that will start the discussion going in the direction you desire. For instance, you might say something like: "Do you use *XYZ* Company's product, and, if so, how do you like it?" Or, "*XYZ* Company has a new product out. Have you heard of it or tried it yet?" If you want to be a little more subtle, you might ask something like: "I hear there's a new product out called .... Has anyone heard of it or tried it?" Questions like these will generate posts from many in the group. You will get a variety of both good and bad comments. People love to give their opinions! Just sit back and watch what happens.

You may want to create your own newsgroup to identify a target group or to set up a focus group. A newsgroup offers a perfect forum for people to talk about your product. Aldus PageMaker has a newsgroup called alt.aldus.pagemaker. All of the discussions on this group are about the Aldus PageMaker product. Posters ask questions about how to use the product and experts provide the answers. Many of these experts have a signature file letting the group know who they are and what their business is. Coincidentally, many of the experts are desk top publishers. You can also use your newsgroups to direct the flow of the discussion to find out particulars you need to know about your product.

Company *XYZ* sells light fixtures across the country. Their brand is well known, but it certainly is not an exclusive business. They created a newsgroup titled alt.light.fixtures and periodically posed questions to the group, e.g., what features do you appreciate most? To this day, the subscribers don't know which company created the group. In fact, a smart competitor would be watching it closely. The point is, people will tell you what you are looking for if you just ask.

To create a new newsgroup of your own, you will want to begin by contacting the newsgroup groups-mentor@amtiahl.com. This is a group of volunteers experienced with the newsgroup creation process. They will help you with the proposal process for a new newsgroup. It is not advisable to try to start a new group until you have some experience with newsgroups first. The recommended time is six months.

You must contact a newsgroup server for their permission to start a new newsgroup. You might want to start with your own provider first. Once you submit your proposal, a vote will be taken by the Usenet administrators of the server you submitted it to. They will determine the merit of your newsgroup.

There are several newsgroups you can subscribe to that will give you some general guidelines. These are: news.announce.newgroups, "How to Create a New Usenet Newsgroup"; news.groups, "Usenet Newsgroup Creation Companion"; alt.config, "So You Want to Create an Alt Newsgroup?" For your benefit, review these before you begin the process of creating a new newsgroup.

SUMMARY

There are thousands of newsgroups on the Usenet. Topics of discussion run the gamut from *Apple* computers to zoology. Almost anything you can imagine is being discussed in one newsgroup or another.

Use the Usenet newsgroups to gather information and do research on your customers, or your competition, find vendors, or screen for employees. Use newsgroups to keep up with financial trends and changes. Create your own newsgroup to communicate with a test group or target group. The thousands of newsgroups available through the Internet can provide you with an abundance of information about all these areas.

COMMUNICATE WITH NEWSGROUPS

1. Lurking will help you find newsgroups with people in your target market.
   a. true
   b. false

2. You should never join in a discussion or try to answer questions in newsgroups.
   a. true
   b. false

3. Newsgroups are just chatter. You won't be able to find any information of value to you.
   a. true
   b. false

4. Just as you're joining newsgroups, your competition is too.
   a. true
   b. false

5. There are so many newsgroups now, no one is allowed to create new ones.
   a. true
   b. false

ANSWER KEY: 1. a, 2. b, 3. b, 4. a, 5. b

3 KEEP IN TOUCH WITH E-MAIL

HOW E-MAIL WORKS

E-mail never takes a holiday. It's not stopped by weather and gets to your address in a matter of moments. You can send mail to anyone in the world any day of the week, including holidays and Sundays, electronically, assuming they have an e-mail address.

E-mail is another direct method you'll use to get information from your customers. It's another of the communication tools of the Internet. You can use it to find target markets or to form focus groups to discuss your product. E-mail provides a way to get your message out to many people at the same time. You'll use the mailing lists of e-mail to do all this.

Remember carbon paper? Before printers it was your best way to get duplicate copies made without having to type them each separately. It sure made it easier to send duplicate letters.

Think back on what it was like before mail merge. You could create the letter once, but you had to copy it for each address and then type each one separately. Mail merge did away with all that tedious, time-consuming labor. Mail merge connects a list of people to a common letter.

Remember the last time you wanted a group of people to hear the same message before the "grapevine" distorted it? E-mail has it! E-mail can create duplicate copies, merge mail lists and more.

With e-mail, you can send a copy of your message to the original recipient and others at the same time. Most of the e-mail software packages will allow you to carbon copy, or blind carbon copy other recipients when sending your message. E-mail makes it easy to send duplicate letters.

Just like with regular mail, it's very important to get the e-mail address correct. If you mistype one number or letter in that address, the mail you're trying to send will be returned to you or sent to the wrong person.

Just as you have an address for your business, you have an electronic address. When you get an Internet connection you will be given an e-mail address. When choosing a name for your address, choose carefully. This address will be on all electronic correspondence you send out. It will also identify you wherever you travel on the Internet. This is your Internet identification.

Many of the same things you do in regular mail you can do in e-mail. You can cc — carbon copy — recipients, set up a mailing list, or add other documents to your mail.

If you wish to create a mailing list, most e-mail packages will allow you to do that. With Eudora, one of the most popular e-mail packages, you have a nickname option for setting up your mailing lists. You choose a name for the list, then type in the addresses for the list in a second box. When you compose a message for the mailing list, you simply type in the name you gave the list and Eudora will send the message to everyone you put in the list when you click on the send button. Setting up your own mailing list will let you do the same thing you do with mail merge, sending the same letter to many people. Because E-mail is instant, you can broadcast your message and use it to beat the "grapevine."

You'll use an e-mail broadcast list the same way you use your address book in "real life." This is your customer base. You own it, therefore, you can send out advertising, surveys, product updates, etc., without fear of reproach. Your biggest concern is making sure you keep this list clean, current, and focused on your needs.

E-mail also has another great benefit to help you in gathering information. It has a tool called "mailing lists." These are groups of people who use e-mail to discuss various topics of interest, much like newsgroups do.

Just like newsgroups, there are thousands of e-mail mailing lists, or "listservs" as they're commonly called on the Internet. You'll find target groups like felines-l at listserv@cornell.edu, that discusses registered cats, huskers at huskers-request@tssi.com that discusses the University of Nebraska sports, or bikecommute at majordom@cycling.org that discusses commuting issues and advocacy. Just like the newsgroups, listservs have their experts. Use them to find experts to help you improve your product or service, or to help you make better informed business decisions.

Here are some more examples of lists you might find helpful: AFinAcc-l at AFinAcc-l-owner@scu.edu.au, which discusses financial accounting, marketing at reynalds@usa.net, which discusses experiences related to marketing a business and customer-support, and atmajordomo@lists.infoboard.com, which discusses how to better support customers, employees and business partners using the Internet. You may want to create your own mailing list for greater customer contact and conduct roundtable discussions of your product.

A QUICK LESSON ON E-MAIL

In order to communicate with the world using your Internet e-mail, you need to know how to use it. The following steps will help you with that.

Step One:	Create a Message. An e-mail message looks very similar to an interoffice memo. You have a "To:" line to insert the e-mail address of the recipient, a "From:" line where your address goes, a "Subject: line," a "Cc: and/or bcc:" line to carbon copy others.
Step Two:	Send an Attachment. You have an "Attachment:" line to let you send an attached document. (see example pg. 42.)
Step Three:	Send to a Group. To create a broadcast list, select Nicknames from the menu options, give the file a name (or nickname) and then add the e-mail addresses you want for that broadcast list file. Type the nickname in the "to:" line of the document you want going to that list.
Step Four:	Forward or Reply to a Message. Select Forward or Reply from the menu options when you wish to forward or reply to an e-mail you've received.
Step Five:	Create a Signature. You have the option to create a signature just as you do with newsgroups. Select Signatures from the menu options and type in your signature information.
Step Six:	Compose Your Message. Compose with thought. Think before you press that Send button.
Step Seven:	Send a Message. Click on the Send button.

MAILING LISTS OR LISTSERVS FOR RESEARCH

Part of the benefits of e-mail is a service called a mailing list, or listserv, as you'll see it more often referred to. A listserv is a program that manages mailing lists. Mailing lists on the Internet are similar to newsgroups in that you have people with like interests discussing topics of concern to them. The difference is that listservs are more immediate and whenever one person posts to the list everyone on the list gets the post whether they want it or not. You can use a mailing list very much the same way you use newsgroups.

Like the newsgroups, listservs have thousands of lists falling along the same ranges as some of the newsgroups. To join a listserv you must first subscribe to the list. Subscribing to a list involves sending an e-mail message to the list administrator with the message in the body "subscribe <list name>" (without the quote marks). To find a list of lists, you can go to sites on the World Wide Web like Liszt Directory of E-mail, Discussing Groups at **http://www.liszt.com**, Tile.Net/Listserv at **http://www.tile.net/tile/listserv**, or **http://www.NeoSoft.com/internet/paml**. Using these search tools, you can find lists on topics such as: BizNews News Service Business News Releases, cybernet Franchise and Business Education, entrepreneur issues for people who want to own their own business or pbs-users for users of Publishing Business Systems Software.

The Internet has four major mail list sites:

1. List Proc
2. MajorDomo
3. Mailbase
4. Mailserve

In addition, many universities have their own mailing lists. Each list operates similarly, and provides computer horsepower for your business. Although you could manage a list on your own computer, due to the time, security, memory and capacity required to handle a mailing list it is not advised. For a nominal fee or even no fee, you get the convenience without the work.

You can scan these lists of lists and find one that deals with an area that you are interested in for your business, or that holds a particular group of people that would fall into one of your target groups. Subscribe to those lists then sit back and read the mail that comes in. If you choose to participate, you can follow the same guidelines we outlined for you in newsgroups. Use your signature file to let them know who you are, and answer their questions with examples of how your business would have, or did, handle that same problem.

You can subscribe to a couple of listserv lists to assist you in the research you're doing on accounting for small businesses. Read through the posts each day and keep the ones that will help you most or answer questions you have about the subject. When you have a question that the group can help you with, post it to the list, then sit back and absorb all the information you receive.

Lists provide a perfect venue for conducting questionnaires or assessing customer attitudes. Here's how you can do original research using a listserv:

- Identify 4–9 questions you want to ask and make sure they can be answered easily.
- Create your survey.
- Contact the list administrator, or owner, and offer the survey as an example. Promise to share results with the group.

If you ensure that the survey results are of value to everyone, few if any will balk at using the list for this purpose. It will, in fact, meet the original purpose of the Internet!

Mailing lists can provide you with an abundance of information. They can also help you increase your customer base and add to your business mailing lists. But do not send a survey or questionnaire to the mailing list as a whole until you receive permission from the listserv administrator first. Mass mailings even in listservs are frowned upon and can be grounds for having you removed from the list. Keep in mind that the Internet has a different philosophy of doing things than what you find in the "real" world. Play by their rules, written and assumed. You will get much further and have more success.

KEEP IN TOUCH WITH E-MAIL

1. E-mail lets you send a message to:
   a. only one recipient at a time
   b. multiple recipients
   c. only to the original recipient and a copy to one other person

2. With e-mail you can:
   a. send copies to numerous recipients
   b. add documents to your mail
   c. both of the above

3. You can create your own e-mail mailing list.
   a. true
   b. false

4. Listservs on the Internet:
   a. are similar to newsgroups
   b. are more immediate than newsgroups
   c. everyone on the list gets the posts
   d. all of the above

5. You can create a survey or questionnaire for research.
   a. you can post it to any list and get positive results as long as you clear it with the list administrator first
   b. first you should create 25–100 questions
   c. create questions that require time and thought from the group
   d. keep all the results to yourself

ANSWER KEY: 1. b, 2. c, 3. a, 4. d, 5. a

RESEARCH WITH E-MAIL

E-mail is the most popular and most powerful tool on the Internet. You can use it to conduct all of your research, or you can use it where it's the most effective: to exchange information with your customers. In its basic form, you can use your e-mail connection to communicate with your customers, sending out surveys, product updates, and customer satisfaction questionnaires. They can quickly circle, answer and click again telling you what they want or need, or ask you questions.

A survey is a survey, whether it is distributed by traditional mail or conducted face to face at the mall. Well-constructed surveys gather information effectively. Less thought-out pieces can send you on a series of wild goose chases. An e-mail survey puts your questions online rapidly. Because many people receive upwards of 100 or more e-mail messages a day, you will want to keep your surveys short. You can always do follow-up surveys later. Use your current paper surveys as a guideline, then send it to your mailing list of e-mail addresses.

The advantage to you in sending these surveys via e-mail is that you have no paper costs, no distribution costs and no postage costs. All you have invested, other than your connection, is the time it takes to design the survey.

The advantage to your customer is that you reduce the time he or she has to spend filling out the survey. Because e-mail is immediate and spontaneous, your customer doesn't have to search for a pen, envelope, stamp, or the survey. He or she need only click on the reply button. A computer survey allows the customer to scroll through to the sections that pertains to him or her. The customer simply clicks on a few boxes showing their preference and then clicks on the send button in order to get the survey back into your hands. It's a simple one-time involvement. An e-mail survey allows the customer at one sitting to return it to you quickly and easily.

Your next question is probably, "Where do I get the mailing list for this?" You should be creating your own mailing list from your customer base. Because the Internet is new, and an e-mail address is almost a novelty, your customers, for the most part, will gladly share it if you contact them and ask them to give you their e-mail addresses. You can either have your customer service reps ask them when they call in, or you can include a card for them to fill out and return to you with their payment. Many business and professional people are online already. More are joining daily. Private individuals are also getting connected to the Internet. Just as fax machines are now in almost every business and many homes, the Internet is the next communication tool that is taking over. Eventually, everyone will have an e-mail address.

As you travel the Internet you will also run across people you can collect new e-mail addresses from and add them to your mailing list. You'll find them in newsgroups, list discussion groups and IRC — Internet Relay Chat channels. You'll even get them from your Web site. However, it's always good etiquette to ask permission before you add someone to your mailing list out of hand. Unsolicited mass mailings are still frowned upon in e-mail. For many years the Internet and e-mail had two inviolate rules: no advertising and no unsolicited mail.

Times have changed and the rules eased, but tread lightly. Here are just a few ways you can keep your customers informed about your product or service using e-mail: Exchange product information using electronic mail; send out weekly or monthly product updates or reports to your customer base; set them up in your e-mail package under a mailing list name, and, with the press of a button, you can send your product update to all those people in a matter of minutes.

CREATING YOUR OWN LISTSERV

If you want to establish your own rules, and more directly control the information, you can create your own listserv. One of the best ways to use this listserv feature is to create a focus group and allow members to communicate with each other through your mailing list. List members will each post their comments or questions. You can also start the group going in the direction you want by posting your own questions. The best feature of the listserv is that everyone has the opportunity to respond. It's like having all those people in a room discussing your product. Everyone gets to talk and voice their opinions. However, no one gets interrupted or talked above. Each person gets heard and gets to express their views, while you observe and direct when necessary. Use the list to get your group to tell you everything you need to know.

The best way to identify mail list administrators is to take note. As you are searching for lists, note where most of them are located. Then you can send an e-mail to that address requesting information about how to get a list started. To do this, you would send an e-mail to listserv addresses with the body of the message saying "INFO LISTSERV."

For example, you could send this message to the listserv site at MIT and it would look like this, your "to:" line would say listserv@mitvma.mid.edu, your subject line would be blank and your message would read INFO LISTSERV <your name and E-mail address>.

Another option is to check with your provider. Many providers will offer the option. Whether you choose to use your provider, or a listserv at another site, you will be charged a fee. The fees start at $15 per month. These fees offset the cost of information and space management. There are services that will set up and maintain a list for you. Some of these services are:

- Data Realm Mailing Lists at **http://www.serve.com/list/index.html** They charge $1/megabyte transferred/month.
- Able Data Corp. Mail List Services at **http://emory.com/~emory/able.html** You will need to contact them for their fee schedule.
- Spencer-Davis Group Mailing List Hosting and Administrative Services at **http://www.spencer-davis.com/**. Their fees are 50 to 75 cents per megabyte with a set-up fee of $50 and a $100 deposit.

Setting Up Your Own List Step By Step

To start your own mailing list, you first need to understand the amount of time involved. You will need to commit at least 20 to 30 hours the first week or two for list planning and set up. Then you'll spend between two to eight hours per week on list maintenance.

You'll run your list from your own e-mail account in conjunction with the listserv site. So, familiarize yourself with your e-mailer and how its editor works.

Next you will want to locate a site running listserv software. Check with your provider to see if they offer this service, or note the sites of lists that you have seen. You will need to talk to your provider in either case, since the amount of mail you'll be receiving will increase. They'll need to increase your e-mail storage space. They will probably also charge you for this extra space. This additional fee could start at $30 per month.

After you locate a listserv site, send for their documentation. You'll send the command INFO LISTSERV in the body of your message to the address of the listserv site. Read the information they send you and familiarize yourself with it. This will be the information you need to set up your list, the commands you need and the policies of the listserv site.

To help you through the process of becoming a list owner, there are lists you can join. Two of these are LSTOWN-L@INDY.CMS Technical Help for Listserv Groups and ARACHNET@UOTTAWA Editorial Help for Owners/Editor of Listserv Groups. Subscribe to these groups and use the experts there to help you get your list set up and running efficiently.

Now that you've familiarized yourself with all the documentation and talked to the experts about your listserv site, you're ready to set up your own list. The first thing you need to do is name your group. It's best to use a name with four to eight characters. Take your time and choose a name carefully. And, be sure to check your listserv site to ensure you're not duplicating someone else's name.

Next, you'll need to identify potential members. You'll want to notify your customers, either through direct mail or other forms of advertising. You'll also want to include it in your Web site. Every media piece you create should promote your lists.

Choose the way you want your group members to be able to subscribe. You have two choices — open or reviewed. With open subscriptions, you let members come and go freely, as they wish. This method will allow anyone to subscribe to your list by simply requesting to be added to the list. With reviewed subscription, you decide who you will let subscribe. This method allows you to screen all subscribers. With the reviewed method you can also require potential members to give you information. For example, you could ask them for a statement of interests, or a short bio.

Remember, you will want to qualify leads and flag certain opinions, so think carefully about how to build your list.

You will also want to decide whether or not to moderate the group. Moderating the group will allow you to keep it cohesive and focused. An unmoderated group is totally at the whim of your participants. It will take more of your time to moderate a group, but the benefits of keeping the group focused on your purposes usually outweigh the time involved.

Two other considerations will surface as you start your list: deciding if you'll need more storage space, and whether or not you want to regulate the customer's access to messages. If you're going to use your group primarily for conversation, you won't need extra storage space. However, if you'll be distributing information such as fliers to the group, then you will. You also need to decide if you want nonsubscribers to be able to access and read messages or posts from your group. This is an option you set when you create your list.

Now that you have made all the important decisions about your group, you need to write an introductory document. This document will be sent to all new subscribers and should contain a concise description of your group. It should contain all the guidelines you've established for the group, as well as the purpose, or mission of the list.

Contact the listserv site and arrange to start your group. Notify all your potential members, telling them how and where to send their subscription requests. Start the ball rolling and keep the discussion focused. Your list is now ready to give you all the information you want and need.

Be patient. There is a learning curve to cultivating good information, but within 30 days you should see a significant growth in comfort, and the quality of your content.

USE E-MAIL TO SEARCH OTHER INTERNET SERVICES

E-mail is the most powerful tool on the Internet. Have you ever sent someone to the library to find something for you? Or, called the help desk and asked them a question you needed an answer for? E-mail can be used as a search tool that will act as an unsupervised attendant, finding what you need.

Many universities have search tools called Gopher (electronic programs) that sort through the stacks and find information. You can send an e-mail directly to a Gopher with no people involved and get what you want.

Imagine creating the search message, sending it to the University of Georgia and then going to sleep for the evening. Next morning, what you asked for is sitting in your mail box! Not bad, huh?

You can use e-mail to search almost every service on the Internet. Even if you only have an e-mail connection, you can still use the Internet to conduct your research. It will take a little longer because you will have to wait for your requests to be returned to you, and you will often have to go through more steps in order to get the information you're looking for. In the long run, though, you can use e-mail to search the Internet for resources if that's the only option you have.

Gopher is one of the tools on the Internet that contains files of information. Usually these files are data that's contained in libraries, government entities, medical and scientific research centers, and other such sources. To use gopher via your e-mail, send an e-mail message to: gophermail@calvin.edu, with the body of the message simply saying "help." The response will be a Gopher menu. Choose "Message" from the tool bar and select Reply, then quote the entire message as you received it. You will need to edit the text by placing an "x" next to each item you want information on. You'll then get another response with more Gopher menu items. Keep putting an "x" next to the items that interest you to get the sources you need. This is a easy step-by-step process.

Let's assume you want to look for information on a key word like "lamps." There is an Internet tool that searches out pieces of information in Gopher menus. It is called Veronica. To use Veronica via your e-mail, follow the same steps outlined above, but place an "x" next to the choice that says something about other Gopher servers. Veronica is offered as one of the menu choices, so watch for it. Veronica gives you a very easy way to target your search.

The response will give you a list of Veronica servers. Choose the one nearest you, put the term you want to search for, like "lamps," in the subject line and send the reply. Veronica will respond to you with a list of items that contain your search word. Mark the ones you want and send your list back until you get the information you're searching for.

Another tool on the Internet that contains large files and software or utility programs is called FTP, or File Transfer Protocol. FTP has a search tool at its disposal that helps you to locate files within it. This tool is called Archie. To locate files and retrieve them from FTP, you will want to search with Archie first to find the FTP server the file is residing on.

You know the name of the file you're looking for, but you don't know where it's located. For example, you are looking for a piece of freeware called mIRC. To find it you send an e-mail to archie@archie.rutgers.edu

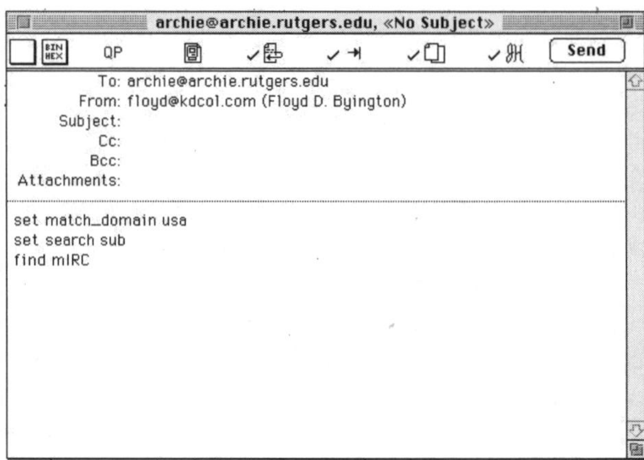

with the message "set match_domain usa" (this limits the search to the US) on the first line without the quote marks, "set search sub" (this limits the search to a filename) on the second line, and "find mIRC" (specifies the search term) on the next line. The response will include a list of files and the FTP sites where they reside.

You've found the site where the software mIRC is located. Now you want to download that software. Using your e-mail, send a message to the e-mail site where the file is listed with the command "open <site name>" on the first line, "binary get <filename>" on the next line and "quit" on the next line. Use binary before the get command only if you are retrieving software programs.

You can even use e-mail to search for posts on newsgroups. For example, you want to find out how people view mutual funds. One of the best ways to do this is to read what people who post to newsgroups have to say about them. To receive a list of newsgroups discussing mutual funds, send an e-mail to netnews@db.stanford.edu with the message 'help' in the body of the letter. You will get a response with information about the various newsgroups offered. Then send an e-mail requesting newsgroup postings containing your key word, "mutual funds."

SUMMARY

E-mail can be your connection to the world. It can also be your greatest resource for information. You can send and receive surveys and customer satisfaction questionnaires, or send out product updates and reports. You can use mailing lists to gather research into a particular area or target group you're interested in. Or you can create your own listserv mailing list for a test product or survey group. If you only have e-mail access, you can use it to search the other tools of the Internet. E-mail can be your connection to the Information Superhighway.

KEEP IN TOUCH WITH E-MAIL

1. E-mail is the most popular and powerful tool.
   a. true
   b. false

2. The advantage to you in using e-mail for surveys is reduced costs.
   a. true
   b. false

3. There is no way for you to create your own rules and more directly control information with e-mail.
   a. true
   b. false

4. You can use e-mail to search almost every service on the Internet.
   a. true
   b. false

5. Listservs can provide you with a tool to set up a test group.
   a. true
   b. false

ANSWER KEY: 1. a, 2. a, 3. b, 4. a, 5. a

4 TALK WITH IRC — INTERNET RELAY CHAT

WHAT IRC IS

Imagine being able to go to an open forum conference, one that has potential customers, market study groups, associates or potential employees. Imagine that you could talk to anyone you wanted, and could ask them any questions. Imagine being able to go from one room to the next, each room full of the kind of people you most need to talk to. One room might hold a group of people all in the 40-year-old age group. This would be a group you would need to talk with to gather market research information — information on how to sell your product to them. Another room might hold a group of experts in marketing or product development. Still another room might hold a group that had qualifications that met your current staffing needs. Now imagine how much better that would be if there were thousands of people at this conference. How much information could you get from these people, if you were given unlimited time to do it?

Internet Relay Chat, or IRC, gives you that potential. It is a service on the Internet that allows you to talk to people online. It lets you use your keyboard and computer to talk in real time to people all over the world. Within IRC there are areas called channels. These are similar to the chat rooms you find on *America Online, CompuServe* and *Prodigy.*

You'll use IRC to find and talk to experts, locate and screen employees, or to talk to target market groups. IRC is another of the communication tools of the Internet and a direct method for researching the Internet. With IRC you go directly to the individual or individually talk in real time. You don't even wait for the posting to be acted on. You simply link up and talk to customers or potential employees. Accessing IRC allows you to set up focus groups and have online discussions immediately. You can conduct "real time" surveys to target groups too.

There are thousands of IRC channels available at any given time. IRC is open 24 hours a day, seven days a week. You can find channels that have people in them that are in the same age group, like channels #35plus, #41plus and #25plus. (The number sign in front of the channel name is how IRC sets up their channels.) There are channels with people from the same city, state or country, like #Texas, #Houston and #Belgium. There are also channels that discuss technical or professional subjects like #win95help, #writers and #dentaltech. Some channels discuss hobbies, religion, music, television shows, sports and, yes, this is another area on the Internet where you will find sex.

IRC can be a great resource for you to get immediate customer feedback. You can create an online forum or focus group that spans the globe, or create tightly focused interest groups in minutes, geographic areas, interests, or age groups. If there's a particular group of people you wish to study, chances are you can find them on one of the IRC channels, or invite them to yours.

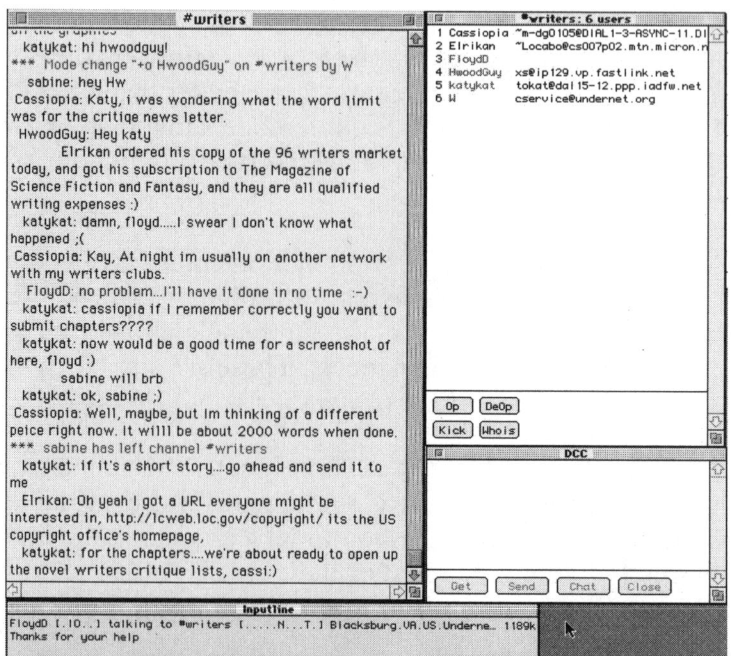

A QUICK LESSON ON USING IRC

Here are a few tips to help you get started using IRC. These steps will help you get connected and maneuver around the chat channels:

Step One: Connect to the "Nets" and Select a Server. To connect to a server, type " /server <the server name>." You may do this also at any point that you wish to change or choose servers. With IRC, the slash "/" tells the program that you are giving it a command.

Step Two: Choose a Nickname. Nicknames are what people in IRC use to identify themselves. Remember the nickname you use will be associated with you and your business, so choose carefully. To give yourself a nickname, type "/nick <nickname>". If at any time you wish to change your nickname, you simply type "/nick <nickname>" without the brackets and press Enter.

Step Three: Join a Channel. To find a channel you'd like to join, type "/list". *WARNING: there are thousands of channels on IRC. Once you have found the channel you like, type "/join #<channel name>", to join that channel. Always include the "#" sign with no space between it and the channel name. Type the channel name exactly the way it appears on the list.

Step Four: Join the Conversation. Type what you want to say. Your message will appear on the channel for all there to see and respond to. (See example pg 46.)

As you use IRC more and more, you will pick up some of the nuances of IRC. Most people on IRC will be more than happy to assist you with any questions or problems you are having. There are also several channels that were set up to help new people, or newbies, as they are called. One of these channels is called "#newbies" another one is called "#ark" and is set up to help *CompuServe* people make the transition from chat rooms to IRC channels. Either of these channels would be a good place for you to start to learn the ropes of IRC.

Some basic commands to help you along in the beginning are as follows:

* /whois <nickname> — use this to find out if someone you know is currently on IRC.

* /who <#channel name> — will tell you who is on that channel.

* /me <your action statement> — will present an action statement, like <nickname> waves to the room.

* /msg <nickname> <your message> — will send a private message to that nickname (private messages can only be seen by the person that you specified as the nickname).

* /part <#channel name> — will take you out of the channel.

* /quit or /bye — will take you completely out of IRC.

* /log <#channel name> — logs the channel conversations.

These commands should help you get a start on your IRC adventures. Don't be afraid to ask questions. Everyone was a newbie for a while, and they remember what it was like. IRC is very dynamic and because you are interacting in real time, give yourself some time to learn this valuable tool.

USING IRC FOR RESEARCH

With all the thousands of IRC channels to choose from, it is an easy task to find a particular target group here. Demographics are easy to locate. You simply choose a channel with a name that will contain the type of people you are trying to target for research. Then you join that channel and observe, join in the group discussions and eventually pose your questions.

You may want to just observe for a while and become accepted as part of the group. Often observing can give you much of the information you need without asking questions.

There are three ways you can begin to survey people using IRC:

1. You can find a channel whose name and purpose match yours and join in the discussion. Go slow until you know these people and have established some rapport.

2. You can create your own temporary group and invite people to join you to discuss and talk about how they would respond to a new product you're developing.

3. You can actually establish your own permanent channel where customers, vendors and employees can meet, greet, cuss and discuss your product. Once you have the floor and information starts flying between people, turn on the log. IRC will create a word-for-word record of what is said, ready to print out.

At some point you will probably want to open your own channel and invite people for a discussion about your product or service. You can invite people you've met on IRC or seen on other channels, or you can entice them by creating a catchy topic line. Each channel is included in a channels list that anyone who logs onto IRC can call up.

Included in this list is the topic line. This is your opportunity to draw people into your channel. Many people choose which channels to join by the number of people in the channel and/or the topic line. More will be discussed about how to set up your own channel a little later on in this chapter.

Some channels can also give you the opportunity to locate potential employees. You or your human resource person can join one of these channels and observe the people there. With IRC you get a picture of the personalities behind the people. If you're looking for a customer service person, the chats can show you which people are good at resolving conflicts, establishing rapport, etc., in the channels. Once you locate a candidate you're interested in, you can take them to a separate channel or to a private conversation and conduct an online interview, much like you would a telephone interview.

Another great use for IRC in conducting your market research is to set up a test group. Create a channel on IRC for the group to meet daily, weekly, or monthly to discuss your test product. This form of teleconferencing allows each person to participate in the discussion much like you would have them do if you were to bring them all together in a room to talk face-to-face. You can monitor and log the conversations so that you have a hard copy of them to present to your marketing or development people.

IRC gives you the opportunity to interact with people all over the country or the world without the expense of mailing, faxing, long distance one-on-one or teleconferencing calls, or bringing people in for conferences. Your marketing people can conduct much of their research using this vast resource of people throughout the world. At any given time there are many thousands of people logged onto IRC. Use this captive audience to talk to more people at one time than a team can talk to in a whole day.

IRC also supports voice communication. You can use software like Powwow or Iphone and use the Internet to conduct voice communication with customers, a focus group, potential employees, or even a target market group. Some of these voice software programs are still in their infancy, but still provide a good way to use the Internet to communicate with people around the world. This method lets you have voice contact without the cost of long distance charges.

Powwow lets up to seven people chat using voice, exchange files, or view Web pages together. Powwow connects users together by their e-mail addresses through IRC. This is how it identifies users. Each user must also have Powwow for it to work.

Iphone will let you have actual voice contact one on one with another user. Long distance charges disappear using Iphone. Iphone uses IRC to connect you to the person you want to talk to, and over the Internet you can talk to people anywhere in the world without the meter running.

THE IRC "NETS"

IRC consists of four different "nets," as they are called there. "Nets" is a vague term that the Internet community uses to designate the various IRC systems. The EFnet is the oldest and most trafficked, the UnderNet is the second largest and was formed as an alternative to the EFnet and its high traffic, Dalnet is third in line with a much smaller base of users, and the smallest and newest is SuperLink.

EFnet usually has an average of 20,000 users online at any time. Being the largest of the "nets," it gives you the best opportunity to talk to more people at a time.

The UnderNet was formed when a group of IR users grew discouraged with the size and volume of EFnet and formed their own "net." It is a smaller and tighter-knit community of users. The UnderNet has an average of 4,000 – 8,000 users online at any time. You'll find many of the same channel names on the Undernet that appear on the EFnet. This "net," although smaller than EFnet, still contains a good concentration of users.

Dalnet began as a role-playing game alternative "net". The average number of users at peak times is under 1,000. SuperLink is even smaller yet, with far few users — often during peak times the number of users is under 500. These two may grow, or other "nets" may be formed as the number of users increases. Using either of these two "nets" will make it easier to gather a group. These two "nets" will let you get a group formed quickly and let them pass information faster. You can get to Dalnet by typing "/server irc.dal.net." To get to SuperLink, type "/server/ irc.superlink.net". You can find the addresses for these servers and the servers for EFnet and the UnderNet in the Index of Internet Sites section of this book.

SETTING UP YOUR OWN CHANNEL

At some point you may wish to set up your own channel to conduct surveys, talk to target markets, or set up a focus group discussion. This is not as difficult as it may sound. On any of these "nets," you can simply start your own channel by typing "/join <#channel name>". <Channel name> would be the name you wish to give your channel.

It's a good idea to check the channels before you start one. Check by typing "/who <#channel name>". This first step of checking will tell you if someone else is thinking like you are, and also keep you from duplicating your efforts. If these channels already exist, join them and learn from their experiences. Don't spend your time and energy making mistakes. The real value of the Internet is the open sharing of information. Don't be afraid to ask questions. If you're not sure how to do something, or if you might be treading on shaky ground, ask. The Internet community is, as a rule, a very helpful and sharing group. Once you've gleaned what you can from existing nets and channels, it's time to set yourself up.

When you create a channel, it will remain open only as long as someone is in the channel. Once the last person leaves, the channel disappears. The more a channel is open the more traffic it will generate. On the EFnet, you can put what is called a "bot" on the channel to keep it open all the time. A "bot" is a self-running program that you can set up to manage a channel for you. Some of the things these "bots" can do is greet your visitors and keep the channel open for you when you're not there. Other commands can be programmed into them to assist you in controlling the channel. Keeping the channel open around the clock has advantages to you.

One advantage is due to the global nature of the Internet. The Internet has users all over the world. Those in different time zones will become familiar with your channel if it's open when they are looking. If you have shifts at your company, you can park someone on your channel to monitor it around the clock. Give them a set of questions to ask visitors.

Another advantage is that if the channel is accessible to people when they need it, they'll keep coming back. If the door's always open they'll feel welcome and want to return. When they feel welcome, they'll tell their friends and bring them to you.

If you wish to have a channel open around the clock on the UnderNet, you must petition the UnderNet organization. They have a group that reviews and approves channel registrations, called cservice. They require the e-mail addresses of at least 10 supporters for your channel for consideration. The Undernet also expects your channel to follow their rules. When they approve the registration of your channel, they will issue you a "channel bot," which is a self-running program. It is owned and run by the UnderNet organization. At this time there is no charge for this service.

When you start up your own channel, you have a couple of options, as mentioned previously. You can designate a catchy title and sit back and wait for visitors to come to you, or, you can invite people you have met on other channels to join you in your new channel by using the "/invite <nickname>" command. Eventually, if you can keep your visitors interested, your channel will grow.

If you are concerned about unwanted visitors, you can also make your channel "invite only," which means that no one can join your channel unless you invite them first. To make your channel invite only, you will type "/mode <#channel name> +i". This is useful if you are conducting an online training session, an interview, or a very tightly focused discussion and don't want to be disturbed. If you're conducting a survey, you'd want to keep people from intruding or interrupting your flow of questions and answers.

Once your channel is open, you'll get visitors, and you'll want to make them feel welcome. Greet them as they come in. Make them feel at home. Then you'll want to start using the channel for the purpose you set it up for — research or market research. Don't club them with questions before they get a chance to settle in.

You can set up a structured discussion. Begin by giving the group a general description of the topic, reasons for it and the benefits to your participants. Begin the discussion and start asking questions and encourage your participants to provide answers. Let the participants discuss their answers and how they differ. You'd use this method to start a focus group talking about your product. Don't forget to turn your log on to keep a record of every discussion.

You can also set the channel up with a moderator. This person will be the only one to ask the questions. You'd use this method to conduct customer surveys. Have your questions prepared ahead of time. Turn the log on so that you have a permanent record of all the answers and who responded.

If you are interested in blazing a totally new trail in customer contact, IRC provides an outstanding vehicle.

SUMMARY

IRC, or Internet Relay Chat, is a great interactive communication tool. It allows you to hold online conversations one-on-one or with groups of people. It's composed of thousands of channels and has many thousands of users connected to it at any given time of the day or night. You will find people there from anywhere in the world.

Use IRC to locate and conduct market research on target markets. Use this vast resource of people from all over the world to get that market and product information. Observe and interview potential employees using this powerful communication tool. Form your own channel and invite people you've met online over to talk about your product and how they use it, feel about it, what they think. Form test groups and create your own channels to let them discuss your product online without the time and expense involved in bringing them all together in one city. Use IRC to its full potential to assist you in making your business grow, to improve your product and to hire the right people for the job.

TALK WITH IRC — INTERNET RELAY CHAT

1. Internet Relay Chat — IRC — lets you talk to people and interview and screen employees.
   a. true
   b. false

2. IRC doesn't let you get immediate customer feedback.
   a. true
   b. false

3. You can locate target groups on IRC.
   a. true
   b. false

4. There is no way to use voice communications with IRC.
   a. true
   b. false

5. There are only two different "nets" for IRC.
   a. true
   b. false

ANSWER KEY: 1. a, 2. b, 3. a, 4. b, 5. b

5 SEARCH THE LIBRARIES WITH GOPHER

WHAT GOPHER IS

Remember when you were in high school or college and had to do a research paper? To do your actual research you had to go to the library, physically search the card catalog by subject and then go to the stacks to find the reference books you needed. Then you had to spend hours hand-writing notes on 3x5 cards, or copying pages out of those books you weren't allowed to check out. Reference books had to stay in the library, so you did too!

Today you can search the files, cut and paste information to your computer and download whole files from hundreds of libraries using Gopher. Gopher is a menu-driven program on the Internet that makes finding information easier and faster than physically searching libraries. All you need to do is identify Gopher sites. Gopher will connect you to *The Library of Congress* and all its information. Gopher can help you find census reports, labor statistics and legislation to keep up to date on employee issues like the Americans with Disabilities Act. You can search weather maps and climate statistics across the country and avoid making travel plan mistakes for your staff. Your training department can access educational programs and learning aids to help prepare training materials, including full power point programs on some things. You can use Gopher to find motivation tips and tactics for your sales people. In addition to all this, you can also find many files to assist you in learning how to use the Internet and its various services.

There are about 5,000 Gopher servers around the world capable of retrieving thousands of documents. It's a program that will wind and twist its way through a maze of files searching for and retrieving the particular piece of information you need. It allows you to access information residing on multiple computers from all over the world. Gopher lets you access information from libraries, databases, universities, research facilities and archives.

A QUICK LESSON ON GOPHER

Here are some steps to help you use Gopher to find what you need:

Step One:	Connect to Gopher. After you click on the Gopher icon, you will get a window to Gopher world. You'll find the various folders and documents of information contained on your Gopher site, like [icon] file folder, [icon] document, [icon] magnifying glass, [icon] graphics, [icon] and binary files. Each of these will have a description of what's contained in that item.
Step Two:	Select an Icon. When you click on any of these items you will open up a file. You may have to keep clicking until you find the information you're looking for. (See insert next page.)
Step Three:	Review the Information. Once you have found the file you're looking for, review the information and either save it or go on. If you wish to save it, simply click on the file menu item, click on Save and give it a file name and directory to save it to your computer.
Step Four:	Continue Your Search. If you don't wish to save the file, simply close it down and continue your search.

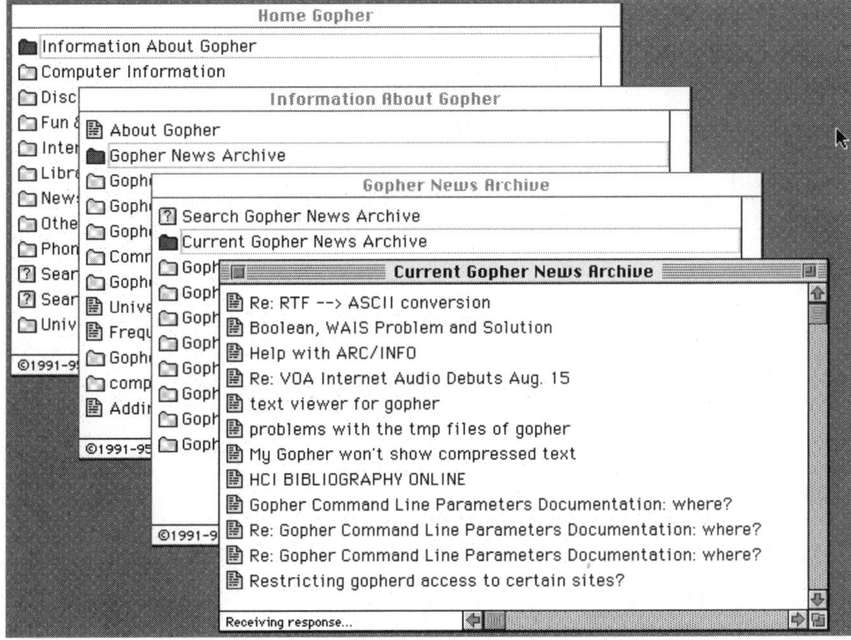

USING GOPHER FOR RESEARCH

Gopher is a powerful resource for almost any kind of information or research you need to help your business. It can help you keep up with the market and job trends in particular areas of the country. It can also bring libraries to your fingertips.

Imagine that you could sit in the *Library of Congress* and find a plethora of information that could benefit you. Imagine being able to find copyright information or governmental legislation that may affect your business. Use it to keep up with environmental issues and avoid costly and hazardous errors to your company by finding the latest laws and legislation . You can even get the phone numbers, addresses and fax numbers of Congressional Representatives. Legal and human resource professionals can search the *Library of Congress* for information about the latest legislation that could affect either business or employees.

If you market your product or service to various parts of the country, or the world, you can even get information about weather conditions, or the types of skills in demand in various parts of the country. If you're considering opening a new plant or store in another area of the country, this is the place you'd go to find out what skills the labor force has there. You can develop campaigns and policies that fit the area, and even identify the people you will be looking at to add to your staff.

Federal and academic job information is also listed on Gopher sites, as well as resumes of people looking for jobs.

Product development, market research, business development and planning departments can use Gopher to get current census reports to help them in planning their strategies. If research has been done for a product you are planning to market or develop, chances are you can find it through Gopher.

Architects can research the University of Michigan School of Architecture for the latest trends that are being offered to students. They can keep up with the changes in their field and also scout out potential additions to their staff by paying attention to the quality of the research papers they find at this site.

Teachers can search out lesson plans, network with other teachers and locate information and sites to share with their students. The Internet and Gopher offer teachers a vast resource of information to excite and help their students to learn. Teachers can also use Gopher to find contests and projects to involve their students in. In short, they will find resources to help them become better teachers.

Your market research team or information management team can keep abreast of the latest trends by reading various magazines and professional journals online through Gopher. Many magazines or excerpts from those magazines can be found online, and complete volumes of certain books are also contained here. You can also search copyrights, trademarks and patents.

Gopher offers your business the resources of thousands of documents, product announcements, magazines, books, libraries, research papers and archives of messages from newsgroups. All this information is at your fingertips, it's easy to locate, and there is either no fee or a nominal fee for all the Gopher information. You no longer need to spend tedious hours in the library searching card catalogs and stacks. Let Gopher search for you.

VERONICA AND JUGHEAD — SEARCH TOOLS FOR GOPHER

There are many Gopher servers available. Some information is contained in all of them, and most of them have files of information that are unique. You can spend your own time searching each of these Gopher sites for what you need. That is, once you've found the addresses to all the Gopher servers that are out there. Or, you can use one of the search tools that were designed to search Gopher for you. Two search tools were designed for just this purpose — Veronica and Jughead. They were designed by college students and, yes, these students had a sense of humor.

Veronica stands for Very Easy Rodent-Oriented Net-wide Index to Computerized Archives, and is a tool you can use to narrow down, or set parameters for searches of various Gopher servers. Veronica allows for quicker and easier searches of all that Gopher space. Veronica lets you search either Gopher menus or document content by specifying keywords to search for. It is a utility to help you identify the location of the pieces of information you are looking for.

To use Veronica, you will need to connect to your Gopher site by clicking on your gopher icon. Then follow these easy steps:

* Locate a menu folder that says Search Gopherspace with Veronica.

* Click on that folder.

* Choose the type of Veronica search you wish to perform, either search by Gopher directories or search by Gopher space (documents). You will also have a choice of locations to search.

* Type in your keyword(s) and click on Search.

* Select the document or file you wish to view.

* Save, print, or close once you are finished viewing.

Using Veronica to search Gopher sites is as simple as clicking with your mouse and typing a few keywords. But the benefit to you in time saved is tremendous. You can even narrow your searches further by restricting how you want Veronica to search for you. This is called Boolean indicators and include the words: "and," "or" and "not." When you include these words in your keywords to Veronica, you are telling her exactly how you want her to search the documents and directories for you. You're narrowing your search parameters.

For example, if you want Veronica to search Gopher for Labor and not Employment, you tell Veronica in your keywords Labor NOT Employment. She will send you back only documents and folders with the word Labor in them. The same applies to the words "and," and "or" when used in your keyword searches.

Jughead is a second tool designed to help you search Gopher sites. It stands for Jonzy's Universal Gopher Hierarchy Excavation and Display. Jughead is very similar to Veronica in how it searches. It differs from her in that Veronica searches documents and folders for your information and Jughead searches menus.

As with Veronica, you can use Boolean search words to narrow your parameters for searches with Jughead. For example, if you wish to search for information on the climate of Maine, you can type it that way. Jughead will add "and" in front of the "of Maine" so that it will search menus containing the words "climate" and "Maine." It will then send you back a report, just like Veronica, listing all the menu items it found within your keyword search parameters. For instance, you would type "climate of Maine" in the search box. Jughead will search for "climate" and "Maine" in all the menus of the Gopher sites. Then it will give you back a report of all the menus that contain the words "climate" and "Maine." Veronica will give you a report back of all the files within the menus with the word "climate" and "Maine" in them.

Many Gopher servers don't include Jughead for searches like they do with Veronica. Here is a list of a few Jughead servers: cwis.nyu.edu at New York University, dewey.lib.ncsu.edu at North Carolina State University, cwis.rice.edu at Rice University and dogwood.missouri.edu at the University of Missouri. These and others will be included in the Index of Internet Sites at the back of this book. However, Veronica is usually provided for you and is such a thorough search tool, you may not have a need to use Jughead. The information is included in the event that you do need it or wish to experiment with it.

You will need to determine which of these tools to use. You'll decide this by what you're searching for, your time involved and what your Gopher server offers you. For instance, your Gopher server may provide you with information about your state, city, or area. Or, if you already know the Gopher site the information resides on, you can go directly to that site. If you're only looking for information within these bounds, using Gopher alone will satisfy your needs.

However, if you don't know the site, you'll want to use either Veronica or Jughead to search for you. You'll use Veronica to search and locate files for you. Veronica will do keyword searches of menus and locate files and documents. Jughead will do a broader-term search and locate menus. You'll then use Veronica to narrow your search. For instance, you would use Jughead to do a broad-term search for pollution. It will give you back a report of all the menus about pollution. Then you'll use Veronica to narrow your search for air pollution in those sites. It will give you back a report of all the files it found with the words air pollution in them.

SUMMARY

Gopher refers to servers that contain files and documents of information. It's a menu-driven program that helps you to find files and documents faster and easier. You will use it to search libraries, directories, magazines and books.

You will use it to locate information on climate and labor statistics for a particular region. You can also use it and its search tools, Veronica and Jughead, to locate particular files of information according to keyword search parameters you designate. You can locate information about your competition, potential employees, product research, weather maps, labor and employment statistics, etc.

Use it to search the *Library of Congress* and keep up to date on the changes in legislation that could affect your business. Search it to find the phone and fax numbers of your congressman, so you can make sure they know how you feel about that legislation they're about to vote on — that legislation you just found on Gopher that could impact your business.

There are over 5,000 Gopher servers you can search to find information to help you and your market research or product development people develop strategies to improve your product, service, or business. Don't spend long hours in the library. Use Gopher to do your research.

SEARCH THE LIBRARIES WITH GOPHER

1. Gopher doesn't make finding information easier and faster than physically searching libraries.
   a. true
   b. false

2. You can search the Library of Congress for:
   a. copyright information
   b. weather reports
   c. none of the above

3. Veronica and Jughead are comic book characters and have nothing to do with Gopher.
   a. true
   b. false

4. Veronica searches Gopher:
   a. by finding documents in Gopher space
   b. by using keywords in its search
   c. both the above

5. Jughead searches menus on Gopher to help you locate documents.
   a. true
   b. false

ANSWER KEY: 1. b, 2. a, 3. b, 4. c, 5. a

6 GET THOSE FILES WITH FTP — FILE TRANSFER PROTOCOL

WHAT FTP IS

At some point you're going to want to move files from another part of the world to your computer. That may sound difficult, but it's not. It's a snap! (Actually, it's a click.) The program that lets you download information is called FTP. FTP stands for file transfer protocol. It was created to promote the sharing of files and transfer data reliably and efficiently.

With access to the Internet, you'll be able to download software and large files, company records and corporate reports. Most files that are contained in FTP sites are very large. You'll be able to get upgrades or add-ons for your favorite software. You'll be able to download product manuals and policy guidelines. Many universities and businesses store vast quantities of files and make those available to the public. You'll also be able to make information available to others with your own FTP site.

There are two types of FTP servers or sites. One is public access FTP and the other is private access FTP. The public access FTP servers are called "anonymous sites." With these anonymous FTP servers, you will log on as anonymous, and when it asks you for your password you will type in your e-mail address. With private access servers you will log on as yourself, usually your e-mail address, and you will be given a password for each private server that you log onto. With these servers you must gain permission to access the files.

A QUICK LESSON ON FTP

It's really not as hard as it may appear. Here are some steps to help you successfully transfer files using FTP:

Step One: Connect to FTP. The software will load and provide you a dialog box to work from. In this dialog box you will select a site to transfer from.

Step Two: Log onto a Site. Complete the boxes in the window if they are not already filled in for you. One of these boxes will ask for your user ID. You will type "anonymous" in this box. All public access FTP sites recognize the anonymous user ID. In the next box type your e-mail address.

Step Three: Select a File. Once the site is loaded you will get a window that displays a list of files contained on that site. Select the file you want to download. Many software programs are contained in pub (public) directories. Also remember to click on the type of mode the file is stored in, like ASCII for text files or Binary for software programs. (see example next page).

Step Four: Transfer the File. Click on the left arrow button. This will transfer the file from the remote system to yours. You will note at the bottom of your screen the file that is being transferred and the status of that transfer.

Depending on when you are downloading, the size of the file and the speed of your modem, this could take some time. For a very large file it could take up to an hour or more to download.

You may also at some time be denied access to an FTP server. Some of these servers have a limit to the number of users they will allow to access them at one time. They will send you a message telling you that they are at maximum access and for you to try later. If you ever run across this you can try later or try another FTP server. There are many "mirror" sites. A mirrored site is one that contains the exact same files as another site, but at a different location. Mirror sites help alleviate the load and promote faster use.

There are various types of files out there that you can download. Each file that is available has three distinct parts to let you know what kind of file you will be getting. The three parts are, the address, the file name and the mode the file is in. Included within each file address is an extension which denotes the type of file it is. Following is a list of file extensions, file types and their retrieval modes:

File Extension	File Type	Retrieval Mode
.c	C programming language source code	Text/ASCII
.com	Executable files for DOS	Binary
.exe	Executable files for DOS, VAX/VMS computers	Binary
.gif	Graphics Interchange Format (compressed)	Binary
.gz	UNIX files that are compressed	Binary
.h	C programming language header files	Text/ASCII
.hqx	Compressed files for Mac computers	Binary
.jpg	Graphics files compressed	Binary
.mpeg,.mpg	Video files	Binary
.ps	PostScript files	Text/ASCII
.sit	Mac files processed by Stuffit program	Binary
.tar	UNIX files in UNIX tape archive format	Binary
.tar.Z	UNIX files that are compressed	Binary
.txt	Plain text files	Text/ASCII
.Z	UNIX files that are compressed	Binary
.zip	DOS files compressed by a zip utility	Binary

If you are unable to find a file you need on any of the sites accessed by your software, you can do a search for files using a search tool called Archie. Archie will be discussed in more detail later in this chapter.

USING FTP FOR RESEARCH

File Transfer Protocol can be used for personal gain or pleasure, like downloading games. It can best be used by business to upgrade your software, get product updates, get sales catalogs, stock information and obtain labor statistics. Anything you need to keep your business automated and current in the marketplace can be found on the Internet. If it's a public access file, you can FTP download it to your computer.

If you are working on a sales or advertising piece, you may need a particular graphics package to complete a job. You can spend hours searching for it in computer stores or you can use FTP to help you find it. FTP can save you time and money in locating software in either freeware, shareware, or full-priced versions of current applications and utilities.

If you're an investment consultant, you must keep up with the latest stock trends. You can wait for the information you need to be made public in the papers. By using the Internet and FTP, you don't have to wait anymore. You can use FTP to download the daily stock listings, keeping one step ahead of your competition.

You can locate your competition's product catalog and download it for review by using FTP. You can also use FTP to make your catalog or product information available to your customers. It also allows you to transfer files from your computer to an FTP server for others in your company to retrieve. If you have numerous locations that aren't connected via a LAN (local area network), this could be a time- and money-saving tool for you.

HOW TO SET UP YOUR OWN FTP SERVER

One of the best ways to make information available to vendors, associates, or customers is to set up your own FTP server. You should first download the FTP FAQ on how to set up a secure anonymous FTP site. You can find this FAQ on the World Wide Web at the following address: **http://sand.edswest.com/reference/nettools/anonymous-ftp.faq**. Then you will need to download the FTP server software. You can find the software at either: **http://www.tucows.com**, or at **http://cwsapps.texas.net**. Some good FTP server softwares are: ITFTP (Integrated Internet FTP), Client/Personal Server, a shareware program, Winsock FTP Daemon shareware program, or FTP Serv-U shareware program.

Setting up an FTP server is not something the average person will be able to do. This is something you will want to pass on to your M.I.S. department. However, there is another option to allow you to offer information for others to download. This is to use your provider. Most providers will include this as part of your package when you sign on with them. They will allot for you a certain amount of space on their FTP server and allow you to upload information to it. If you exceed that allotted space they will charge you a small fee for that extra space. They will usually give you one to two megabytes of space, and if you exceed that space they will charge you around 50 cents per extra megabyte of space that you use. Contact them and let them be your FTP server. Use them to allow you to offer files to your customers, vendors and associates.

SEARCH TOOL FOR FTP ARCHIE — HOW TO USE

There are literally thousands of files on hundreds of systems available to download. Sorting through all the records can often be hard and time consuming, especially if you search each of the anonymous FTP sites yourself. Archie is a search tool that makes finding FTP files easier. It is a program that searches anonymous FTP sites and sends you back a list of addresses of sites that contain the files you're looking for.

Archie searches anonymous FTP file libraries for files. It will give you the host names, the system that has the file, the location, the directory to look for, the size of the file, the date it was uploaded and the name of the file when it gives you a list of sites where your files can be found.

Your provider should furnish you with Archie software. If not, you can find a good Archie software program on one of the World Wide Web locations included in the Index of Internet Sites section of this book.

Click on the icon for Archie, then type in your keyword search. Note: you don't have to have the correct name of the file you are looking for —

Archie will search all the files for ones that contain your keyword, then select the FTP server to search. Click on the Search button. Archie will conduct its search and provide you with a list of sites where your file can be found.

Now that you have your list of sites, you will want to go get your file. Just follow the directions in this section on how to use FTP and substitute a host site from your list for the one in the host name area of the FTP window dialog box. Some good sites to try are:

crvax.sri.com	information and discussions about computer security issues
ftp.cwru.edu	decisions handed down by the U.S. Supreme Court
ftp.ulowell.edu	newsgroups archives
ftp.uu.netlarge	software and newsgroup archive
rtfm.mit.edu	newsgroups and listserv archives
oak.oakland.edu	software archive
ftp.cica.indiana.edu	software archive

SUMMARY

FTP, File Transfer Protocol, is a service on the Internet that contains large files and software or utility programs. It allows you to transfer or download files from a remote system to yours. It allows you to do keyword searches of public and private FTP sites to find files you need.

Use FTP and Archie to locate software upgrades and programs or utilities to keep your computer up to date. Locate your competitor's sales catalog using FTP. Use it to keep up with the stock market. It can be a great source of files to keep you and your business one step ahead.

GET THOSE FILES WITH FTP — File Transfer Protocol

1. With FTP you can:
   a. download files and software
   b. send messages to others
   c. none of the above

2. Downloading files with FTP:
   a. is quick, no matter the speed of your modem
   b. can be done on private servers without permission
   c. can take as much as an hour depending on the size of the file

3. FTP lets you offer files for others to download to their computers.
   a. true
   b. false

4. Archie is a search tool for FTP.
   a. it only searches private FTP servers
   b. it sends you back a list of addresses of sites that contain the files you need
   c. both of the above

5. Archie differs from other search tools because it doesn't search by keyword.
   a. true
   b. false

ANSWER KEY: 1. a, 2. c, 3. a, 4. b, 5. b

7 SEARCH NETWORKS AND DATABASES WITH WAIS

WHAT WAIS IS

You have a medium to large company. You're on a network and have thousands of files in your system. Or, you know of a database you'd like to search. How do you find what you need? WAIS can be your key.

WAIS stands for Wide Area Information Servers. It was designed to help users find and retrieve information from networks and indexed databases. With WAIS you can access personal, company and published information. It was designed to help you find information over a computer network simply by asking questions, including your own company network!

How many times have you wished you could find something inside your own company? Or, have you ever wondered if someone else has already done what you are about to do? Use WAIS to set up your own server and to handle thousands of information sources like spreadsheets, e-mail, databases, etc. Its strength is that it's able to handle a wide variety of databases like plain text, images, sounds, or spreadsheets. WAIS will organize, index and search your company's information. You can also use it to allow your customers to search within your company for information you will make available to them.

You'll also use WAIS to search other Internet databases, like bibliographical databases, to find publications about your industry, or service guides. You can use it to search online library systems to find books and reference materials on new techniques in your field that could improve your product or service.

You'll use WAIS to let your human resource people search for Environmental, Health and Safety documents, and to help you reduce the risk of legal actions from employees. You'll use it to keep up to date on NAFTA (North American Free Trade Act) and you'll also use it to find cultural material about areas of the country or world you plan to expand into.

WAIS will search newsgroups or listserv archives to find market research information that was there before you got access to the Internet. You can also use it to search for journals, like computing or electronic journals. Keeping abreast of industry trends is now fairly easy!

WAIS can help your company index and search e-mail. It can store, index and search company resumes, proposals, sales videos or promotional literature, and having WAIS makes it possible for your customers to search a database you set up for them containing catalogs or marketing literature.

A QUICK LESSON ON WAIS

To help you use WAIS to search for information contained in one of the many databases or networks accessible through the Internet we have included these steps to help you:

Step One: Connect to WAIS. Then select the database to search. If you don't already know of a database to search, you can use WAIS to find one for you. You simply type the words "Directory of Servers".

Step Two: Enter the Keyword. With WAIS you can use natural language questions or Boolean searches.

Step Three: Review the Report. WAIS sends you back a report with a brief description of each document it found. These documents will be listed in the order of their relevance to your question.

Step Four: Select the Document. Review the list of documents and select the document. WAIS will retrieve it and display it on your screen.

With the 400 plus WAIS databases available, you don't want to search all of them for your information. You must determine which sources are more likely to have that information. To do this you will want to search the master database of WAIS services — The Directory of Servers — for the name of sources on your topic. Use a general topic, like Pollution. Select a source from the ones that show up in your report and repeat your search, narrowing the parameters in your topic.

For example, you've found a source dealing with Pollution. You will then type in that source in the database search area, then you can narrow your search by asking WAIS to search for Air Pollution.

HOW TO BECOME YOUR OWN WAIS SERVER

It's easy to become a WAIS network server. All that is required are the following components:

* A database of information that you want to make available.
* The WAIS server software.
* A TCP/IP network to connect users to the server.
* An Internet connection (optional).

Keep in mind that you will only want to make available a collection of information that you want the public to have access to over a computer network or the Internet.

You will furnish the database. The WAIS server software will create an index to assist in the fast search and retrieval of your data. It also supplies the search engine, a query reporting facility, tools for restricting access and monitoring usage and the WAIS protocol for communicating with users. You can find WAIS server software at one of the sites listed in the Index of Internet Sites section of this book.

If you wish to set up your own WAIS server, there are WAIS-compatible programs available for most operating systems. Since the WAIS system uses a protocol or language based on industry standards, servers can communicate with WAIS-compatible program users regardless of the user's operating system, or vendor.

TCP/IP (Transmission Control Protocol/Internet Protocol) is an industry-standard protocol or language used to transfer information between computers. The Internet is based on the TCP/IP network. It provides a very wide and broad audience for network servers. If you wish to publish your information only to networked clients internal to your organization, you won't need Internet access. Most businesses begin by using WAIS within their company alone and later move to external publication over the Internet.

When you choose to set up your own WAIS server, you will want to be able to have a record of the users and their activities on your server. The WAIS server lets you do this because it automatically records all transactions in a log file. It records the server's process identification number, the current number of transactions performed for this user, the date, the time and the type of transaction. It records six transaction types:

* Opening a connection.
* Searching a database.
* Returning results from a search.
* Retrieving a document.
* Closing a connection.
* Errors and warnings.

WAIS can make it easier for you to search and retrieve documents from your own or other's databases or networks. It can also give you a record of all searches performed by you and others searching your databases.

USING WAIS FOR RESEARCH

There are hundreds of publicly registered WAIS databases on the Internet. Use WAIS to access and search them. You can also use it to find and retrieve formatted documents, like phone listings and repair manuals, contracts, status reports, or marketing materials.

Use WAIS to access the online public access portion of a library system, or to access MARC records to retrieve bibliographic material, citations, or full-text articles and even fully formatted publications.

WAIS will also let you search through personal or group e-mail archives. During a search, WAIS will return the subject line of the mail messages most relevant to your question, and then deliver the appropriate mail message. Imagine being able to search every letter and memo your business has created for a specific client in moments.

DATABASES ON THE COMMERCIAL SERVICES

From time to time, you're going to want to get information that is only contained on databases. The commercial online services like *CompuServe, America Online* and *Prodigy* have some very good databases. These commercial online services can often be your only resource for these databases.

For instance, *CompuServe* has one of the best bibliographical databases you can search. It's called *Knowledge Index,* and is a database that makes available several bibliographical book and magazine databases. However, many of these databases have limited hours of operation. So plan your searches ahead of time, because the commercial services will also charge you an hourly fee for using these databases. For example, *CompuServe* charges $24 per hour extra to use Knowledge Index.

These commercial online services have discussion groups similar to newsgroups on the Internet, called forums. Many of the forums will also archive their discussions. These databases of discussions can be an excellent resource for research into areas of interest for you, or into what your competition is doing.

Although the commercial services don't provide full Internet access, each one has their own unique advantages, and different services they offer to their subscribers. You will need to ask friends and associates what each one offers and determine which of these services has something that could benefit you or your company. Any one or all of them could be a great resource of information for you. Each one has distinct subscribers who could provide you with targeted market research.

Questioning friends or associates who have one or more of these commercial services will give you the best information on what each of these services has to offer. You might even want to ask them to show you around the service they're using. This will let you see first hand what each service has to offer. Then you can choose which service has the kinds of information you need to research.

DATABASES ON THE INTERNET

The Internet is one of the most comprehensive sources for databases. Universities, libraries, businesses, the scientific community and the government have many databases available on the Internet. One of the biggest and best is the *Library of Congress.*

Gopher and the World Wide Web along with WAIS will be your best places to begin your search for databases. Gopher we already know contains the *Library of Congress* as well as many others. There is also a site on the World Wide Web that is a database of over 10,000 business organizations. It and other indexed database addresses can be found in the Index of Internet Sites section of this book.

If you know which database you want to search, your job is half done. Your next step will be to find the right tool to search that database, Gopher, World Wide Web or WAIS. If you don't know which database to search, you can always do a keyword search in any of these Internet services to locate one of the many databases available.

SUMMARY

WAIS allows you to search the hundreds of publicly accessible databases and networks available on the Internet. You can also set up your own WAIS server to make searching through your own databases easier and quicker. Or, you can set up your own server and make particular databases available to your clients. WAIS allows you to use natural questions, Boolean operators and relevance feedback to narrow your searches and give you back a report of the documents it found based on their relevance to your keyword search. It will also generate a report log of the users that accessed your database, complete with times, dates, and types of searches they did. It is a powerful tool to search indexed databases and networks for information.

SEARCH NETWORKS AND DATABASES WITH WAIS

1. WAIS is a tool you can use to:
   a. organize, index and search your company's information
   b. search other databases
   c. all of the above

2. You can use WAIS to find repair manuals, contracts, status reports or marketing materials.
   a. true
   b. false

3. WAIS has no way to let you search through personal or group e-mail archives.
   a. true
   b. false

4. The commercial online services can sometimes be your only resource for certain databases.
   a. true
   b. false

5. There are only a few databases available on the Internet.
   a. true
   b. false

ANSWER KEY: 1. c, 2. b, 3. b, 4. a, 5. b

8 GET TO PLACES WITH TELNET

WHAT TELNET IS

Imagine having your own personal librarian. Someone who will go to all the libraries for you. This librarian would know where to search and how to use all the catalogs at each library, and she would be able to go places you can't get to. Wouldn't it be nice to have someone like this and not have to pay any extra for them? Well, you do — it's called Telnet.

Telnet is your personal librarian. It will let you log onto a remote computer and let your computer search as though it were that computer. It will let you access libraries and bulletin board systems all over the world. It will let you access systems via the Internet that you wouldn't otherwise be able to get to.

Use Telnet to get into databases and bibliographies. Use it to search the General Accounting Office Documents database to find information to keep your accounting and bookkeeping department up to date and to find innovative ways to improve your accounting system.

Let your librarian, Telnet, search the Software and Courseware Online Reviews database to find documentation and reviews on software. Use it to help you find the best software to improve your system, or help you locate courseware to use in training your staff.

Telnet has access to and can search the World Bank Socio-Economic Data database to keep your business up to date on national and world trade and financial policies. Don't be left with second-hand information. Telnet is designed to keep abreast of the world.

Use Telnet to connect to Freenets and Community Computing Systems. It can search the General Bulletin Services to find an industry-related service, like Dentistry-Online. Telnet will search local departments of labor for information about the unemployment rates or labor pool and laws for any area of the country, and, you can get Telnet to help you keep up to date on privacy rights changes and laws by searching the Privacy Rights Clearinghouse Bulletin Board Service.

Keep up to date on changes in network systems and management by searching the various databases on the Network Information Services. Or, use Telnet to help you locate colleagues or experts by searching directories or white pages using Whois/Whitepages/Directory Services.

Let Telnet search the American Institute of Law Libraries Information Service to help your human resource or legal department keep abreast of legal changes that could impact your business. Use it to help you make the right decision for your company when purchasing electronics by searching the Biotechnet Electronic Buyers Guide database. Let Telnet help you get started in a new business venture by searching the Business Start-Up Information Database. Don't let the *IRS* find you lost and confused. Access their IRIS Internal Revenue Information Services database to find information on tax law changes.

Use Telnet as you would a personal librarian. Use it to get to places that aren't readily accessible using the other Internet service tools. Use it to reach information to keep you on the fast track!

A QUICK LESSON ON TELNET

Telnet is your connection to distant places. Use these lesson steps to take you to those places:

Lesson One: Connect to Telnet. Click on the Telnet icon. If you don't already have Telnet, you can download it at: **http://www.tucows.com or http://cwsapps.texas.net**.

Lesson Two: Open a Connection. Select Open a Connection from the menu options. You'll then be asked to provide the address of the computer you want to connect to. You'll use Hytelnet to help you find these addresses. (Hytelnet will be explained in the next section.)

Lesson Three: Log in. At the prompt you will need to type your username and password. Many of these sites will require that you have an account with them. Contact them either through e-mail or telephone to set up an account.

Lesson Four: Issue Commands. You can run a program by typing its name and pressing Enter. Or, follow directions and search for your files.

Lesson Five: Log off. Be sure to log off each system when you are done.

USING HYTELNET TO FIND PLACES TO GO

Your librarian needs an assistant to help her find the libraries to search. This assistant for Telnet is called Hytelnet. It's a search tool you'll use to locate libraries, bulletin board services and databases for Telnet to access.

You'll need to download the software to be able to use this tool. You can find Hytelnet through FTP at, ftp.usask.ca, in the directory pub/hytelnet. Or, you can download it from the World Wide Web site at: **http://www.cc.ukans.edu/hytelnet_html.tar.z**.

Once you have it loaded and set up on your system, you'll start it by typing "hytelnet". You'll be given a menu which will list the references, like Library Catalogs, Other Resources, or Miscellaneous Resources available for Telnet. Use your arrow keys to move around in these references.

Select your reference and scan the list of resources for the one that best suits your needs. For example, you could choose Other Resources and then select Databases and Bibliographies to find the address for General Accounting Office Documents. Once you've found your address you can start your Telnet session from Hytelnet by pressing the right arrow or "y."

Hytelnet will give you most of the information you need for each site to be able to use Telnet successfully and find the information you need. It will give you the commands you need once you're connected to use with the system you'll be Telnetting to.

Use Hytelnet's databases of Telnet sites to help you find the sites to let Telnet help you find what you're looking for. Use Hytelnet as an assistant to your personal librarian, Telnet.

USING TELNET FOR RESEARCH

Telnet is your personal librarian. Send her out to places you need information from. Use Telnet and its assistant, Hytelnet, to find those places for you. Let Telnet get you to places you can't find on the Internet.

Use Telnet to keep up to date on socio-economic changes in the financial marketplace by searching the World Bank Socio-Economic Data database. Use this resource to keep up with the world of finance, banking and trade.

Let Telnet help you find out the best software or electronics to purchase by searching the Software and Courseware On-line Reviews, or Biotechnet Electronic Buyers Guide databases. Don't continue to use outdated materials to train your staff. Use the Courseware On-line Reviews to help you find the latest training materials.

Don't send your traveling staff into unknown weather conditions. Use Telnet to research weather conditions at the National Climate Data Center Online Data Systems. Before you relocate, find the experts in that area to help you with that relocation by searching Real Estate On-Line.

Outsmart the *IRS* and make sure you have the most current tax laws by searching the IRIS Internal Revenue Information Services databases. Make sure your accountant is completing your tax return and filing your taxes within the current laws.

Find experts and improve your data processing department by searching the Data Processing Independent Consultant Exchange. Use this resource to make sure your data processing department is state of the art.

Ensure that you're familiar with international trade laws and policies by searching the International Trade Information Services databases. Find the experts to help you expand your business into the international trade arena.

Don't overstep your bounds when dealing with the public or your employees. Search the Privacy Rights Clearinghouse Bulletin Board Service and communicate with experts in this area. Keep abreast of changes in this sensitive area.

Keep up to date with industry trends and changes by searching Carl System Databases for professional journals. Find out what your industry is doing and what your competition is facing by researching these journals.

Let your legal department or human resources people keep abreast of changing laws by searching the Constitutional Documents database or the American Institute of Law Libraries Information Service database. Don't be caught out in the cold with no recourse. Use these databases to ensure that you're not infringing on your customers' or employees' rights. Make sure you know the current legislation that could impact your company.

Telnet to places you can't normally reach otherwise. Use it to find information to improve or protect your business. Use it to help you make better informed business decisions.

SUMMARY

Hytelnet will help you find resources to use with Telnet to find information that could help your business. Use Telnet to go to libraries and bulletin board services. Use it to keep abreast of changes in laws and legislation that could affect your company. Use it to find experts to help you improve your business or in relocation. Use Telnet to find resources and experts to help you improve your data processing department, or to help you outsmart the IRS. Let Telnet help you start a new business or expand into international trade. Let it help you make sound business decisions and keep on the fast track!

GET TO PLACES WITH TELNET

1. Telnet:
   a. will let you access systems via the Internet that you wouldn't otherwise be able to get to
   b. cannot log onto remote computers
   c. only gives you second hand information

2. There is no search tool for Telnet.
   a. true
   b. false

3. Hytelnet:
   a. helps you find sites for Telnet to access
   b. gives you the commands you need to use with the system Telnet connects you to
   c. both of the above

4. Telnet has no way to help you improve your business.
   a. true
   b. false

5. Telnet will let you find experts in the fields of:
   a. data processing
   b. real estate
   c. both of the above

ANSWER KEY: 1. a, 2. b, 3. c, 4. b, 5. c

9 INTERACT WITH CUSTOMERS USING THE WORLD WIDE WEB

WHAT THE WORLD WIDE WEB IS

Imagine the business possibilities if you could be open 24 hours a day, have a branch in every major city, and you had a way to personally respond on the spot to any customer inquiry. The World Wide Web gives you these possibilities. It lets you have a store front that's available to customers 24 hours a day, no matter where they live in the world. You no longer have to limit yourself to your local, regional, state or country area. You can use the World Wide Web to offer your business, product or service to everyone in the world.

The World Wide Web was created in 1989 so that researchers could share information. It uses a special language called Hypertext. Originally, these Web documents were text only. Then, in 1993 a Web browser was designed. The invention of the Web browser expanded the capabilities of Web documents. With Web browsers, the World Wide Web became multimedia, as users added graphics, sound and video.

Web browsers are to the World Wide Web what Windows are to DOS. Remember how with DOS you had to type out commands to get things done? Remember how difficult it was to remember the right sequence of commands to get things done in DOS? Sometimes you had to type in long strings of letters and numbers that make up these commands. If you don't have a very good memory, you had to keep a notebook with these commands in it so you could refer back to them when you needed them.

Windows took those long commands and turned them into point-and-click functions for the mouse. Windows simplified using your computer. Web browsers took the commands of Hypertext language and made them point-and-click Windows compatible.

At about the same time that Web browsers were designed, the public and businesses gained access to the Internet. Businesses put a new face on the Internet and the World Wide Web in particular. It's where businesses are now going to advertise and promote their products and services. It's also where you will go to research your competition to find out what they're doing and what they're saying to their customers. You'll use it to find your competition.

Just as every person who has a connection to the Internet is given an address (usually their e-mail address), every Web page on the World Wide Web has an address. They are called URLs, pronounced "yurls," which stands for Uniform Resource Locator.

There are literally millions of addresses or documents on the World Wide Web, just like there are millions of books in the libraries around the world. However, searching for information on the World Wide Web is much easier and faster than searching for information in a library. We will go into more detail on how to search the World Wide Web later in this chapter.

Businesses, institutions or individuals can have more than one Web page to present their information. Because the World Wide Web is not a linear format like books, Web site owners can have many pages of information of varying sizes containing their information. Each one of these separate pages can, and often does, have separate addresses, thus creating the millions of pages of documents on the World Wide Web.

A QUICK GUIDE TO THE WORLD WIDE WEB

The following lesson steps will help you access and navigate your way around the World Wide Web:

Step One: Connect to the Web. To make the World Wide Web work you need two things: a good browser and a good search tool. (Search tools will be detailed in the next section.) Click on the icon for your browser. Many providers have their home page load for you when you connect to the Web browser. This is a good opportunity to find out what your provider is doing in your community as well as some of the other users on your provider. Some of them could very well be your competition. (See insert next page.)

Step Two: Fill in the Address. If you already have an address you want to go to, you will type that address into the "Go to:" box provided by your browser. Be sure to type the address exactly as it was given to you. Web browsers are also case sensitive. Try connecting to some of the sites we've mentioned in this book.

Step Three: Use Search. Choose a search tool. There will be several search tools you can choose from. Lycos, Yahoo, Web Crawler and InfoSeek are four of the most popular. Type in your keyword and press "Search".

The browser will allow you to go back to any document or site you have been to previously by clicking on the back button at the top of your browser window. This will save you time in reviewing all the documents that your search will locate for you. Keep in mind that many of these documents are quite large. Unless there is a very pressing reason to save a document, you may wish to simply bookmark the site so that you can get back to it easily at a future date, rather than save it on your hard drive. Let the owner of the document keep it on his hard drive and free up space on yours.

All the browsers have a feature that allows you to bookmark a site. This is very similar to what you do when you are reading a real book. If you find an area that you want to come back to, you slip a piece of paper in that place or fold the corner down before you close the book. The bookmark feature of browsers let you click and save the site's address into memory. Then, when you want to come back to that site later, you simply click on your bookmarks and click on the saved site. The browser will find the address and load the site for you.

As you can see, this is much easier and quicker than spending long, tedious hours in a library. With the click of a mouse you can search through the millions of documents contained on the World Wide Web.

SEARCH TOOLS/ENGINES — WHAT THEY ARE AND HOW TO USE THEM

There are various search tools, or search engines, as they're sometimes called, to help you search the World Wide Web. All these search tools were designed to make your searches easier. They allow you to quickly search the millions of documents on the World Wide Web.

Search tools came about as an indirect method to organize the information contained on the Web. The first search tool began as a project to organize all the information and documents on the World Wide Web. Because there was so much information already, and more was being added daily, this project was abandoned and replaced with one to search all those documents for information.

This project resulted in a tool that would search all the documents on the World Wide Web by a keyword or words. The search would generate a report of all the documents it found with those keyword(s). Now, all search tools use this same keyword basis for their searches. Each varies in how they present their search reports to you. There are dozens of search tools available for the World Wide Web. We are going to discuss the four major ones here. For your benefit, we've listed their addresses along with a few of the others in the "Index of Internet Sites" section of this book.

Yahoo Search Results

Found 173 matches containing **cad**. Displaying matches 1-25.

Matching Yahoo Categories

Business and Economy:Companies:Computers:Software:Computer Aided Design (***CAD***)

Business and Economy:Products and Services:Computers:Software:Computer Aided Design (***CAD***)

Matching Yahoo Sites

Arts:Architecture:Institutes

- University of Kentucky College of Architecture - **CAD**, Architect, Sustainable, Urban Condition.

Arts:Computer Generated:Artists

- Macey, Paul - Aerospace **CAD** images & MPEG animations galore!

Business and Economy:Companies:Apparel:Manufacturing:Directories

- Fashiondex, Inc - apparel manufacturing companies listed by category: notions,trims, dyeing, and **CAD**.

Business and Economy:Companies:Architecture:Consulting

- Federal Street Architects - Federal Street Architects offers on line **CAD** design from archaeological and historical to single family residential sites

Yahoo was the first search tool that was designed. When you type in your keyword(s) and click on the search button, Yahoo gives you a search result report that lists all the documents it found. It lists these documents by category. Each document in the list will include the title of the document and a brief description of the document. When you click on the title of the document, Yahoo will load the document for you to view.

Yahoo will allow you to define your search options. It will allow you to indicate whether you want it to show matches that have at least one of the keywords (Boolean or), or all the keywords (Boolean and). You can tell it if you want it to consider the keywords to be substrings or complete words. You can also indicate how many matches per page you want to see, either 10, 25, 50, or 100.

Lycos is another good search tool. When you type your keyword(s), Lycos gives you a search result report that lists the documents it found. Each of the documents on the lists includes the title of the document, a brief description of the document and the address of the document. Again, if you click on the title of the document, Lycos will load it for you to view.

Click on graphic to visit site.

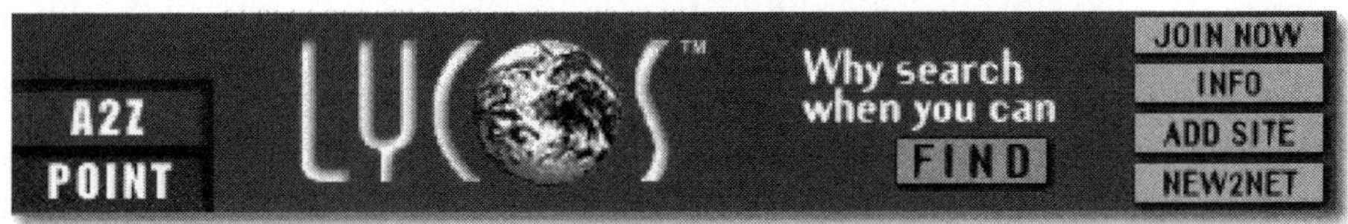

Lycos is hiring. Examine the exciting opportunities at Lycos.
Check the facts - read the Web Catalog Size report.

Lycos search: Bullfrog

Lycos Feb 25, 1996 catalog, 25892915 unique URLs

Found 458 documents matching at least one search term.
Printing only the first 10 of 55 documents with at least scores of 0.010.

Found 5 matching words (number of documents): bullfrog (458), bullfrogg (4), bullfroggy (1), bullfrogs (89), bullfrogt (4)

---

1) ***EPI Center / EA WEB*** [1.0000]

Abstract: Thank You for Visiting the EA Web! All files are copyrighted © 1995 Electronic Arts If you have any problems viewing our pages
http://www.ea.com/bullfrog.html (1k)

---

2) ***Yahoo - Business and Economy:Companies:Computers:Software:Games:Bullfrog*** [0.9016]

Abstract: Business and Economy : Companies : Computers : Software : Games :**Bullfrog** Options * **Bullfrog** [EA Web] * **Bullfrog** [Official] - The Place for **Bullfrog** info, for games, hints tips etc...
Copyright © 1994-96 Yahoo! All Rights Reserved.
http://www.yahoo.com/Business_and_Economy/Companies/Computers/Software/Games/Bullfrog/ (2k)

---

3) ***Yahoo - Business and Economy:Companies:Computers:Software:Games:Bullfrog*** [0.9009]

Abstract: Business and Economy : Companies : Computers : Software : Games :**Bullfrog** Options * **Bullfrog** [EA Web] * **Bullfrog** [Official] - The Place for **Bullfrog** info, for games, hints tips etc...
Copyright © 1994-96 Yahoo! All Rights Reserved.
http://beta.yahoo.com/Business_and_Economy/Companies/Computers/Software/Games/Bullfrog/ (1k)

Lycos will also allow you to define your search options. You may choose to match some terms (Boolean and), match any terms (Boolean or) or match 2, 3, 4, 5, 6, or 7 terms. You may also tell it whether you want a loose, fair, good, close or strong match. You can define the number of results per page to either 10, 20, 30 or 40. You can also tell it if you want a standard or detailed summary of results.

Webcrawler is another search tool you can use. When you type your keyword(s), Webcrawler gives you a search result that only lists the documents it found. To find out what is contained in each document, you will have to click on each title. Webcrawler will then load that document for you to view. To define your search options with Webcrawler, you have the options of finding all or any words, and returning 10, 25 or 100 results per page.

At the moment, InfoSeek is the only fee-based search tool. They charge you a minimum fee for their services. However, they only charge you a fee if you use them as a full-service search tool. It's still a fine search tool without utilizing it to its fullest potential. When you type in your keyword(s), InfoSeek gives you back a search report that lists the documents it found. It gives you the title of the document and a brief description of what's contained in the document. If you click on the title, InfoSeek will also load the document for you to view. It also lets you define the search options by choosing what area of the Internet you wish to search, like all Web pages, newsgroups, Usenet FAQs, or reviewed pages.

These search tools will help you to find the information you are looking for quickly and easily. They will also reduce your research time drastically.

INTERACT WITH CUSTOMERS USING THE WORLD WIDE WEB

1. With the World Wide Web:
   a. you can have more than one page
   b. pages aren't linear like books
   c. each page can have a separate address
   d. all of the above

2. A Web browser:
   a. can save you time by letting you go back to documents already viewed
   b. doesn't have any way to mark documents, like a bookmark, so you have to save them
   c. none of the above

3. Search tools for the World Wide Web:
   a. were designed to organize all the documents on the WWW
   b. generate reports of all the documents it finds with your keyword(s) in them
   c. both of the above

4. Yahoo was the latest search tool that was designed.
   a. true
   b. false

5. Lycos is the only fee-based search tool.
   a. true
   b. false

ANSWER KEY: 1. d, 2. a, 3. b, 4. b, 5. a

USING THE WORLD WIDE WEB FOR RESEARCH

You can use the World Wide Web to research your competition or find the information you need for product development. Use it to research market trends, find software and utilities, or get financial information. You can even read magazines and newspapers on the World Wide Web. You can use it to get information from your customers, or give them information about you. You can now do your research in a fraction of the time it used to take you, by using the World Wide Web.

It is a vast resource of information. Since the World Wide Web is where businesses are going to promote their product and services, you will more than likely find your competition here. If your competition has an Internet connection, chances are you can search for them on the World Wide Web and see what they are doing, how they are presenting themselves to the public and what they're telling their customers.

Research papers abound here, as well as scientific papers. Universities and the scientific community created the Web and used it to exchange information. They still do. If the research has been done and a paper written about it, you'll find it on the World Wide Web. If the product you're trying to develop has had any component or part designed by someone else, you can look in the World Wide Web to find the research they did. Use it to research what's been done to find out how you can make improvements.

You can also use it to see what the industry standards are. There are many publications and organizations on the World Wide Web that contain valuable information concerning your industry. Use the search tools to find them.

Many of the major magazines and newspapers have a Web site on the World Wide Web. You can now read these online. You can use them to keep current with national issues. If you don't have the time to review these online publications, there are clipping services you can subscribe to that will search them for you. These work much the same way they do in the "real" world. The only difference is that they search the online publications. They will also search listservs and newsgroups for you. You tell them what you are interested in and they will do keyword searches of all the publications, lists and newsgroups. They will then e-mail you a report with their findings, or, if you like, they will provide a file for you that you can retrieve at your convenience.

Much of the information you get online is more current than what you get either through your local or national newspapers or television. *Dow Jones,* for instance, has a Web site. The information you get online is posted as soon as it is available, whereas your local or national papers and television have to rely on reporters to receive the information. They have to produce or print it, and then it has to be viewed by you. This often results in delays of days and hours at the minimum.

In Chapter 1 we talked about using customer surveys to gather information about your customers. You can create your own Web site or let a consultant do it for you and include your customer survey in it.

Your home page or Web page is your starting point on the World Wide Web. It's your principal point of presence. It should be designed for exploration of your business and its capabilities, like a corporate resume.

In planning your Web page, begin with a goal — decide on a main purpose for your page. You must have definite ideas about what you want your Web presence to accomplish, like advertise, sell, gather information, or build your corporate image.

Advertising is the number one reason most businesses establish a presence on the Web. You must be especially creative in this medium. Create a useful service to draw people in, and then create a place they want to stay once they get there.

There are several elements that are very important to include in your Web page design. These include the title, logo, size and graphics. Used correctly, these elements will help your customer identify with you, find you using search tools, load your site quickly and stay there when they get there.

Use meaningful, eye-catching and informative titles. Don't omit them or use obscure titles. Use a title that will help your customer find you. Many search tools search for keywords in the titles of Web pages. So, the title you choose needs to be one that will bring your customer to you.

Use the logo or trademark you use in all your other advertising. You

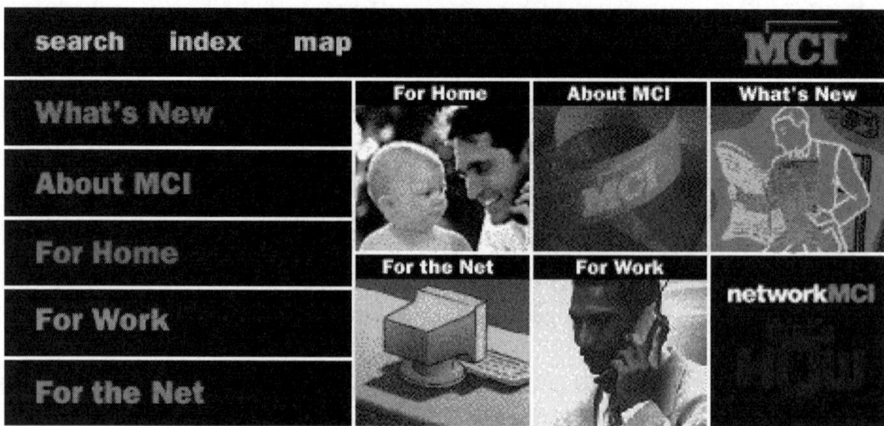

Thursday, February 29, 1996

From the MCI Newsroom

SENATOR MCCAIN PRESS SECRETARY TO JOIN MCI PUBLIC POLICY COMMUNICATIONS STAFF

Welcome to the new MCI Web site.
Our goal is to provide you with the consummate Internet resource for all of your telecommunications needs. Here you will find the latest announcements from MCI and information about the company, our products and services, and our solutions for your residential and business needs. Current and future MCI customers can take advantage of useful online services. For starters, there's customer service online for MCI Customers.

Go where you need to go with networkMCI paging. Need to send a page? You can send a text or numeric page online right now!

want your customer to be able to recognize and identify with you. Keep your Web page design consistent with your traditional advertising efforts.

The World Wide Web isn't linear like books are. Pages can be all different sizes. You want to create pages that are attractive and easy on the eyes — not too much text all together — and that make it easy for your customer to find what they're looking for. For instance, you can link your table of contents to the pages they reference. This will allow your customer to jump around in your site, sort of like they would if they were wandering around in a store. Use multiple smaller pages to make it easier and faster for your customers to load them and read them.

You don't want to use oversized graphics. The larger the graphic the longer it takes your viewer to load your pages. If it takes too long for customers to load your document, they'll go elsewhere. And, of course, your graphics should tie into your business, product, or service and should be of interest to your viewers.

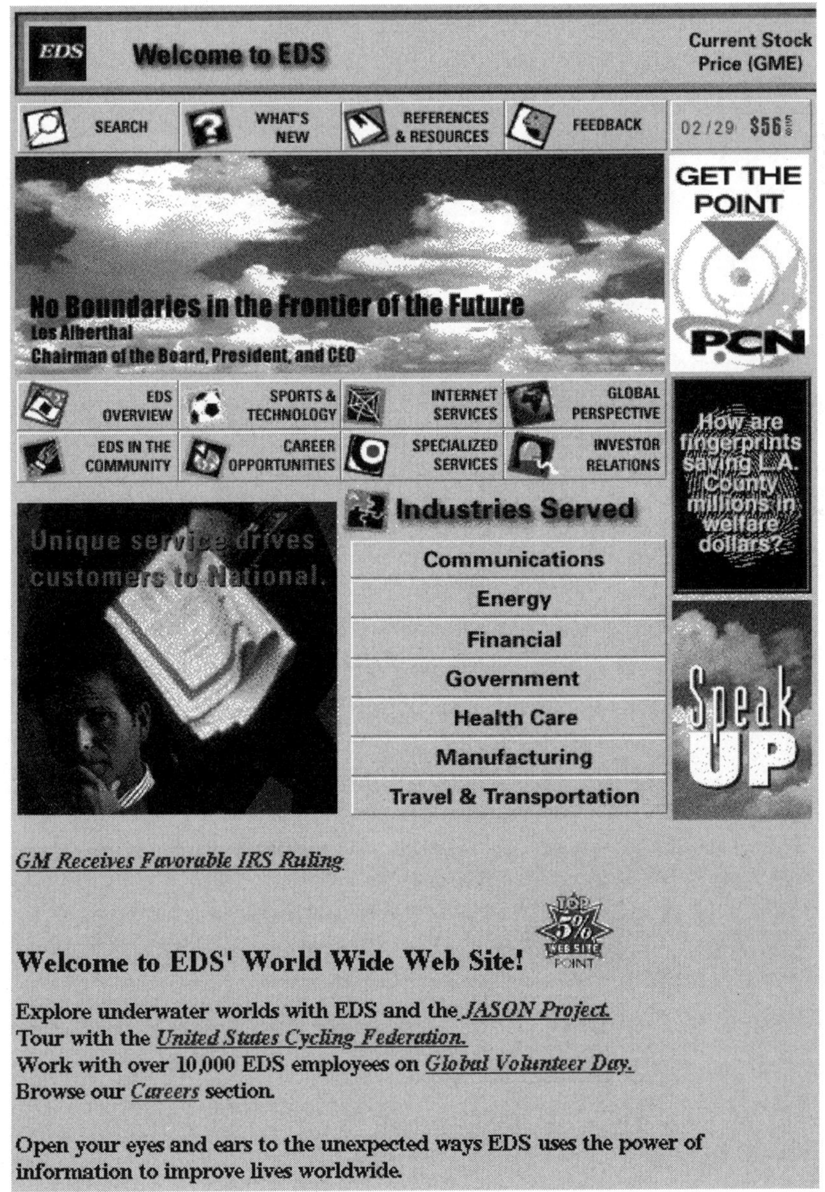

Use your Web pages to tell your customer about your business, product, or service. Use the World Wide Web to build your image to your customer. Use it to sell your product. You can include your sales catalog here and update it in a flash to keep products in it that are of value to your customers, and eliminate the ones they aren't interested in. Let them order from you online through your Web site.

Use it to gather information from your customers. Include surveys, contests, sweepstakes and giveaways to attract customers, and then use it to get them to give you information about themselves. The potential of Web pages to increase your sales, help your business to grow and to get information to help you improve your product or service is limitless.

Including a customer survey in your Web pages will get your visitors to give you the information you need. You will also reach more people using this method, due to the high volume and diversity of users on the Internet. As an added benefit, you'll have a constant record of the results, saving you time and money hiring a team to tally the results of these surveys.

As we discussed in Chapter 1, there are services that will design and/or manage customer surveys for you. They will maintain and analyze the results for you also. One such group is called Data Star Inc. You can find their address in the "Index of Internet Sites" section of this book.

You can also use Web pages to bring visitors to you, much like you would a special promotion in your store. Offer games, giveaways or contests to attract visitors. Then, use tracking software to tally the number of visitors you attracted. Combining that with the number of sales you received works the same here as it does in the physical world. You can also set these games, giveaways and contests up with an area for the customer to provide you with basic information about themselves.

With the millions of documents that are available on the World Wide Web, you will be able to find almost anything you are looking for there. The search tools that have been designed for the World Wide Web make that job easier and faster than it ever was before, and much easier and faster than traditional means of research.

The World Wide Web lets you keep a finger on the pulse of the world. You can keep up with the changing trends in the marketplace. Use it to find out what the competition is doing and what's being done in your industry and with your products.

SUMMARY

Just as libraries around the world contain thousands or millions of books and publications, the World Wide Web contains millions of documents. Many of these documents are about businesses. You can probably find your competition here. You can find out what they're doing and what they're saying to their customers. Use it to get your customers and visitors to give you information.

With these millions of documents, you can find almost anything you're looking for, from industry standards to market and finance trends and research papers. You can also use clipping services to search all the publications and listservs for your areas of interest. Use this powerful multimedia tool to create your own Web site and include customer surveys. Use the search tools that were designed for the World Wide Web to find the information you're looking for. Don't spend tedious hours in a stuffy library. From the comfort of your home or office, use your mouse, computer and the World Wide Web to do your research.

INTERACT WITH CUSTOMERS USING THE WORLD WIDE WEB

1. You won't be able to find your competition on the World Wide Web.
   a. true
   b. false

2. Many of the major magazines and newspapers have a Web site on the World Wide Web.
   a. true
   b. false

3. Pages on the WWW can be different sizes.
   a. true
   b. false

4. Oversized graphics load fast and impress your visitors.
   a. true
   b. false

5. You can use Web pages to bring visitors to you.
   a. true
   b. false

ANSWER KEY: 1. b, 2. a, 3. a, 4. b, 5. a

10 CONCLUSION

The Internet is huge. It contains millions of files of information. It has millions of users. Use it to get the information you need to make you a better decision maker. Use it to help you improve your business, to improve your product, or to improve your customer service. Use it for what it was designed for — to share information.

Use the Internet and its various tools and services to get information about your customers by using direct methods like the communication tools of e-mail, IRC and newsgroups. Interact with your customers and let them tell you what you need to know. Use the World Wide Web to get information indirectly from them by using software that tracks the number of visitors to your site, or by offering games, giveaways and contests that will require them to provide background information on themselves.

Use newsgroups to find target groups and listen in on their discussions. Use them to do your market research. Offer advice and answer questions and establish a bond that will allow you to work in questions of your own without offending the group. Use them to find experts to keep you better informed and help you make better business decisions. Keep abreast of market or finance trends by joining one of the various newsgroups. Newsgroups give you the opportunity to find vendors, suppliers and even employees. Set up your own newsgroup and use it for target or focus group discussions of your product.

Use e-mail to keep in touch with your customers and get information from them. Send out customer surveys or let your customers relay their questions or comments to you using e-mail. Subscribe to mailing lists of discussion groups and use them to give you an interactive source of limitless research. Use the listservs to set up a focus group and let them have an interactive discussion of your product or service.

Use IRC (Internet Relay Chat) to spontaneously interact with the Internet community. Join various channels to find target groups, potential employees, etc. Use the thousands of users to get market research information. Set up your own channel and interview employees or target group members. Or, set up a channel to allow a focus group to have a round table discussion about your product or service. Use your print media to advertise your channel.

Use Gopher to search libraries, universities and repositories quickly and easily. Use the search tools for Gopher — Veronica and Jughead — to help you find menus and files of information. Search the *Library of Congress* for information on your legislators or laws that could have an impact on your business. Use Gopher to get climate and weather conditions around the world. Have your human resources people use it to get labor statistics and keep current on labor laws. Use Gopher to find materials to motivate and train your staff. Use it to find out more about the Internet.

Keep your computer system up to date using FTP (File Transfer Protocol). Download the newest versions and upgrades of software with FTP. Locate and download your competition's catalog or product updates. Use FTP to work in conjunction with vendors, clients or advertising agencies to exchange information, saving you both time and money.

Create your own WAIS server and use it to index and search your own databases. Or, let your clients use it to access the information you make available to them. Use it to search the Internet indexed databases and networks for the information you need. There are databases in abundance on both the Internet and the commercial online services. Find the ones that you need using WAIS and use them to your advantage. Use the tools of the Internet and WAIS to search those databases. Ask friends and colleagues which online services have which databases and what they have to offer. Choose the one that best suits your needs and use them to their full potential to give you the information you need.

CONCLUSION

Use Telnet and its assistant, Hytelnet, to go to places you can't find on any of the other Internet services. Let Hytelnet find the site address then let Telnet take you there. Use them to find information on areas that will help you improve your business and make better informed business decisions. Use Telnet to search databases and keep abreast of changing laws that could affect your business. Use it to keep one step ahead of the *IRS*.

The World Wide Web is the place businesses are going now to promote themselves and their products. Use it to find out what your competition is up to and how they're presenting themselves to the world. Use the World Wide Web to offer your customer surveys to visitors. Find out what the public thinks about your company, product or service. Use the search tools of the World Wide Web to search the millions of documents available on it. Use the search tools or engines of the Web to quickly and easily search for new product developments in your industry.

The Internet is a versatile tool. The various services and tools it has to offer can provide you with an abundance of information. Each tool has its own unique function and information offerings. Sometimes that information overlaps. No matter what service or tool you use, you are almost guaranteed to find information on just about any subject you need or want.

The Internet is a vast resource of information. Learning how to use it can greatly reduce the time and tedium you're used to doing in traditional research at libraries. Use the Internet to get information about your customers, your competition, product development, laws and legislature. Happy hunting!

INDEX OF INTERNET SITES

Most of the sites that will be included here will be World Wide Web sites. In Chapter 8 we discussed addresses or URLs. Included here are those addresses. Type these into the "Go to:" box of your browser and press Enter. Your browser will connect you to the site and load it for you. For the software sites, you will be able to download the software simply by clicking on the piece of software you want. It will be highlighted and will download as soon as you click on the highlighted words. Many of the files will be zipped, or condensed files. You will need a program that will unzip them. These too can be found on one of the software sites.

SITES FOR SOFTWARE

Stroud site: http://cwsapps.texas.net/
This site contains many *shareware and freeware versions of some very good software and utilities. They rate the software they offer by stars.

Tucows site: http://www.tucows.com
This site contains shareware and freeware versions of software and utilities. It rates the software using cows. The rating is based on ease of use and reliability.

Shareware Central site: http://shareware.com
This site has over 160,000 shareware and freeware versions of software. They also have a newsletter you can subscribe to that will update you on new releases. This site also contains many programs for Mac users. It is also a searchable index of software.

* Much of the software that is available on the Internet is either freeware, meaning just that — free, or shareware, meaning you have to pay for it, but the price usually ranges from $29–$49.

Jumbo, The Official Web Software Site: http://www.jumbo.com
This site has over 49,000 programs.

World Gain: http://interax.com/~stav/wg_free.htm
Place to get free software, services and training.

The Well Connected Mac: http://www.macfaq.com
Tools and toys for Mac users.

Netscape: http://www.netscape.com
Mosaic for Windows: http://www.ncsa.uiuc.edu/SDG/Software/Mosaic
Mosaic for Macs: http://www.ncsa.uiuc.edu/SDG/Software/MacMosaic

Any of the pub. sections of any anonymous FTP sites will contain software, either freeware or shareware. Here are a few of the better ones:
ftp.cica.indiana.edu — Indiana widows archive
oak.oakland.edu — Oakland University
wuarchive.wustl.edu — Washington University archive

NEWSGROUP RESOURCES

DejaNews search tool: http://www.dejanews.com
This tool searches newsgroups by keywords you indicate.

InfoSeek search tool: http://www.infoseek.com
You can define your option for searches by selecting the search newsgroups option.

Usenet Info Center: http://sunsite.unc.edu:80/usenet-b/home.html
Everything you want to know about Usenet.

Newsgroups group: news.group
Lists every Usenet newsgroup.

WinVN Newsreader: http://www.ksc.nasa.gov/software/winvn/winvn.html
A popular freeware Usenet newsreader.

Guide to buying and selling on the Internet: rec.answers or news.answers
Infinite Ink's Newsgroup search site.

http://www.jazzie.com:80/ii/internet/newgroups.html
This site links you to newsgroup search tools and lists with descriptions.

Usenet news finder: http://www.nova.edu/Inter-Links/cgi-bin/news.pl
Searches newsgroups by subject.

Anchorman site: http://www.ph.tn.tudelft.nl/People/pierre/anchorman/Amn.html
Browse newsgroups by hierarchy or subject, also tells you how many groups exist in each hierarchy.

Newsgroups used as examples:

misc.consumers, misc.business.consulting, misc.business.credit, misc.business.records-mgmt, misc.taxes, misc.invest.stocks, rec.crafts, rec.boats, rec.hunting, rec.skiing, soc.religion, soc.support, soc.genealogy, soc.culture, sci.med, sci.engr, sci.energy, news.announce.newsgroups, news.misc, news.groups, comp.databases, comp.home.automation, comp.networks, comp.security, alt.genealogy, alt.smokers, alt.left-handed, alt.real-estate-agents, alt.mothers, alt.new-england, alt.architecture, biz.books.technical, biz.comp, biz.general, biz.comp.accounting, biz.marketplace

LISTSERV SITES

Listwebber site: **gopher://www.lib.ncsu.edu:80/hGET%20/staff/morgan/listwebber.html**
Searches list archives.

Publicly accessible lists:
http://www.NeoSoft.com:80/internet/paml/bysubj.html
Arranged by subject.

Thousands of lists:
http://scwww.ucs.indiana.edu/mlarchive/
More than 11,254 listservs from 308 sites.

New lists: usenet at
bit.listserv.new-list

Listserv archives: gopher —
sjuvm.stjohns.edu
then select disabled; listserv

Mail list services:
http://www.polaris.net/~daxtron/daxindex.htm

Liszt Directory of E-mail Discussion Groups:
http://www.liszt.com

Interlink's Interest Group Finder: **http://www.nova.edu/Inter-Links/cgi-bin/news-lists.pl**

Tile.Net/Listserv: http://www.tile.net/tile/listserv

More lists of lists:
http://andomedia.einet/GS/lists.html
http://www.lsoft.com/lists/listref.html

List Administrators

Data Realm Mailing Lists:
http://www.serve.com/list/index.html

Able Data Corp. Mail List Services:
http://emory.com/~emory/able.html

Spencer-Davis Group Mailing List Hosting and Administrative Services:
http://www.spencer-davis.com/

Listserv addresses mentioned in Chapter 3:
LISTOWN-L@INDY.CMS, ARACHNET@UOTTAWA - LIST OWNER LISTS
Discussion Group for Cat Owners — Felines-L at listserv@cornell.edu
Financial Accounting Discussion Group — AFinAcc-L at AFinAcc-owner@scu.edu.au
Sports Discussion Group — huskers at huskers-request@tssi.com
Commuting Issues Group — bikecommute at majordomo@cycling.org
Marketing Discussion Group — marketing at reynalds@usa.net
Customer Support Discussion Group — customer-support at majordomo@lists.infoboard.com

IRC SERVERS

for the EFnet:
irc.mcs.net
irc.colorado.edu
irc.eskimo.com
irc. texas.net
irc.virginia.edu
tramp.cc.utexas.edu

for the undernet:
austin.tx.us.undernet.org
manhattan.ks.us.undernet.org
bloomington.in.us.undernet.org
davis.ca.us.undernet.org
SanJose.CA.us.undernet.org
norman.ok.us.undernet.org
okc.ok.us.undernet.org

oak.oakland.edu.us.undernet.org
phoenix.az.us.undernet.org
pittsburgh.pa.us.undernet.org
ann-arbor.mi.us.undernet.org
Blacksburg.VA.US.undernet.org
washington.dc.us.undernet.org

for Dalnet:
irc.dal.net

for superlink:
irc.superlink.net

GOPHER SERVERS AND SITES

gopher.tc.umn.edu — all the world's gophers listed by country and continent

liberty.uc.wlu.edu — Washington and Lee University WLU more gopher sites

sunsite.unc.edu — Sun Microsystems and the University of North Carolina

riceinfo.rice.info — organization of gopher resources

gopher.unt.edu — University of Texas gopher

library.cpl.org — Cleveland Public Library gopher

garnet.msen.com — job resource gopher

wiretap.spies.com — electronic books to government documents

ericir.syr.edu — all aspects of education

info.umd.edu — U. S. Census excerpts

gopher. cic.net — gopher, K-12 resources

ashpool.micro.umn.edu — weather resources

libra.arch.umich.edu — Univeristy of Michigan School of Architecture

Jughead Server: gopher.psi.com:2347/7-t1 — PSINET

Jughead Server: comics.scs.unr.edu:800/7-t1 — University of Nevada

Jughead Server: liberty.uc.wlu.edu:3002/7 — William and Lee University

FTP — FILE TRANSFER PROTOCOL — SITES AND RESOURCES

Newsgroup site: alt.sources.wanted and alt.answers

List of anonymous FTP sites.

Newsgroup sites: alt.sources.wanted and alt.answers

List of anonymous FTP sites.

Australian mirrored software archive: archie.au

Gopher software info: boombox.micro.umn.edu

Virus information: ftp.nevada.edu

Software archive: ftp.ulowell.edu

Usenet archives:rtfm.mit.edu — list of Usenet newsgroups and FAQs

Indiana Windows archive: ftp.cica.indiana.edu

Oakland University archive: oak.oakland.edu

Washington University archive: wuarchive.wustl.edu

Computer Security Issues: crvax.sri.com

Supreme Court Decisions: ftp.cwru.edu

Software and Newsgroup archive: ftp.uu.net

Archie Servers:

archie.ans.net — New York

archie.sura.net — Maryland

archie.rutgers.edu — New Jersey

archie.unl.edu — Nebraska

How to set up an FTP server FAQ:

http://sand.edswest.com/reference/nettools/anonymous-ftp.faq

WAIS SERVERS AND SITES

http://gort.ucsd.edu/jj/wais.html

http://www.wais.com/directory-of-services.html

http://www.wais.com/wais-dbs/

http://www.ncsa.uiuc.edu:8001

ftp.cnidr.org — WAIS software

INDEXED DATABASES

New Market Forum, 10,000 business groups database: **http://www.newmarket-forum.com/**

Genealogical Database Index: **http://sillyg.doit.com/genweb/**

Rockefeller U. Computing Services Database: **http://www.rockefeller.edu/rucs/rucs.db.html**

National Pest Management Materials Database: **http://info.aes.purdue.edu/ipmdg.html**

Chemical and Biochemical Databases: **http://www.chem.surrey.ac.uk**

Astronomical Databases: **http://www.star.le.ac.uk:80/databases/**

TELNET RESOURCES

Software sites:

http://www.lights.com/hytelnet

ftp.usask.ca

http://www.cc.ukans.edu/hytelnet_html.tar.z

WORLD WIDE WEB SEARCH TOOLS

Yahoo: **http://www.yahoo.com**

Lycos: **http://www.lycos.com**

Webcrawler: **http://www.webcrawler.com**

InfoSeek http:: **http://www.infoseek.com**

Excite: **http://www.excite.com**

AltaVista: **http://www.altavista.digital.com**

OpenTextIndex: **http://www.opentext.com/omw/f-omw.html**

AllInOne: **http://www.albany.net/allinone/**

NlightN: **http://www.nlightn.com**

WWW Virtual Library: **http://www.w3.org/hypertext**

Galaxy: **http://galaxy.tradewave.com**

Clearinghouse for Subject-Oriented Internet Resources Guides:

http://www.lib.umich.edu/

Inktomi: **http://inktomi.berkeley.edu**

WORLD WIDE WEB SITES USED IN EXAMPLES OR REFERRED TO

CBS: **http://www.cbs.com**

Internet America: **http://www.iadfw.net**

Lycos Home Page: **http://www.lycos.com**

Data Star Inc: **http://www.std.com/datastar/electr.html**

MCI: **http://www.mci.com**

EDS: **http://www.eds.com/home.html**

SURVEY DEVELOPMENT AND ADMINISTRATIVE SERVICES

Info Quest Internet Surveys and Statistics: **http://www.teleport.com/~tbchad/stats1.html**

Surveys on Demand: **http://www.winternet.com/~connie/**

Campbell Development Surveys: **http://www.ncs.com/cds/**

MST Surveys: **http://www.mstnet.com/MST/surveys.html**

General Index

Aldus Pagemaker, 25

Alta Vista, 20

America Online, 45, 79

Archie:
- using with e-mail, 42
- using with FTP, 71-72

Boolean operators, 62, 81, 96, 98

"Bots," 52

Channels, 45-53

Commercial databases, 79-80

CompuServe, 45, 48, 79

Customers:
- questionnaires, 11, 36
- surveys/polls, 5-8, 36, 46, 49, 53, 107

Dalnet, 51

Data Star, Inc., 8, 104

DejaNews, 20

DOS, 91

EFnet, 51

E-mail:
- creating your own listserv, 37-41
- finding posts with, 43
- how it works, 29-30
- listserv, defined, 31
- mailing lists, 31, 33-36
- listserv providers, 38
- search tools, 41-42

Eudora software package, 30

FAQs, 20

Forums, 79

FTP (File Transfer Protocol)
- defined, 67-70
- file types, 67
- researching with, 70
- search tool (Archie), 71-72
- searching with e-mail, 42
- setting up, 70-71
- sites, 72

Gopher:
- defined, 57
- researching with, 59-60
- search tools, 61-63
- use with E-mail, 41-42

Hypertext language, 91

Hytelnet, 85, 86, 88

InfoSeek, 98

Internet:
- databases on, 75, 78, 80
- direct/indirect access, 6-12
- history and definition, 1-4

Iphone, 50

Knowledge Inc., 79

Library of Congress, 57, 59, 64, 80, 108

Lycos, 93, 97-98

MARC records, 79

mIRC, 42-43

Newsgroups:
- categories of, 17-19
- creating, 25-26
- defined, 15-16
- "lurking" on, 23
- posts, 16, 20-23, 43
- search tools, 19
- signatures, 20-21
- subscribing, 16
- threads, 20, 23

Nicknames, 48

Powwow, 50

Prodigy, 45, 79

SuperLink, 51

TCP/IP, 78

Telnet:
- defined, 83-85
- researching with, 86-88
- using with Hytelnet, 86

UnderNet, 51-52

URLs, 92

Usenet, 15-16, 26

Veronica:
- using with e-mail, 41-42
- using with Gopher, 61-63

Web Crawler, 93, 98

WAIS:
- becoming a server, 77-78
- defined, 75-77
- researching with, 78-79

World Wide Web:
- advertising on, 10-12, 101-104
- bookmarking, 94-95
- defined, 91-93
- researching with, 100-105
- search tools/engines, 95-98
- Web browsers, 91-92, 94-95

Yahoo, 93, 96

Buy 3 get 1 FREE!

60-MINUTE TRAINING SERIES™ HANDBOOKS

TITLE	RETAIL PRICE	QTY.	TOTAL
8 Steps for Highly Effective Negotiations #424	$12.95		
Assertiveness #442	$12.95		
Balancing Career and Family #415	$12.95		
Change: Coping with Tomorrow Today #421	$12.95		
Customer Service: The Key ... Customers #488	$12.95		
Dynamic Communication Skills for Women #413	$12.95		
Empowering the Self-Directed Team #422	$12.95		
Getting Things Done #411	$12.95		
How to Conduct Win-Win Perf. Appraisals #423	$12.95		
How to Find Your Way Around the Internet #4305	$12.95		
How to Manage Conflict #495	$12.95		
How to Manage Your Boss #493	$12.95		
Listen Up: Hear What's Really Being Said #4172	$12.95		
Managing Our Differences #412	$12.95		
Master Microsoft® Word #406	$12.95		
Motivation and Goal-Setting #4962	$12.95		
A New Attitude #4432	$12.95		
PC Survival Guide #407	$12.95		
Parenting: Ward & June ... #486	$12.95		
Peak Performance #469	$12.95		
The Polished Professional #426	$12.95		
The Power of Innovative Thinking #428	$12.95		
Powerful Leadership Skills for Women #463	$12.95		
Powerful Presentation Skills #461	$12.95		
Real Men Don't Vacuum #416	$12.95		
Self-Esteem: The Power to Be Your Best #4642	$12.95		
SELF Profile #403	$12.95		
The Stress Management Handbook #4842	$12.95		
Supreme Teams: How to Make Teams Work #4303	$12.95		
The Supervisor's Handbook #410	$12.95		
Team-Building #494	$12.95		
Techniques to Improve Your Writing Skills #460	$12.95		
The Windows Handbook #4303	$12.95		
The Write Stuff #414	$12.95		

Sales Tax
All purchases subject to state and local sales tax.
Questions?
Call
1-800-258-7248

Subtotal	$
Add 7% Sales Tax *(Or add appropriate state and local tax)*	$
Shipping and Handling *($1 one item; 50¢ each additional item)*	$
Total	$

VIP No. 705-008438-096

VIP No. 705-008438-096

Buy 3 get 1 FREE!

60-MINUTE TRAINING SERIES™ HANDBOOKS

TITLE	RETAIL PRICE	QTY.	TOTAL
8 Steps for Highly Effective Negotiations #424	$12.95		
Assertiveness #442	$12.95		
Balancing Career and Family #415	$12.95		
Change: Coping with Tomorrow Today #421	$12.95		
Customer Service: The Key ... Customers #488	$12.95		
Dynamic Communication Skills for Women #413	$12.95		
Empowering the Self-Directed Team #422	$12.95		
Getting Things Done #411	$12.95		
How to Conduct Win-Win Perf. Appraisals #423	$12.95		
How to Find Your Way Around the Internet #4305	$12.95		
How to Manage Conflict #495	$12.95		
How to Manage Your Boss #493	$12.95		
Listen Up: Hear What's Really Being Said #4172	$12.95		
Managing Our Differences #412	$12.95		
Master Microsoft® Word #406	$12.95		
Motivation and Goal-Setting #4962	$12.95		
A New Attitude #4432	$12.95		
PC Survival Guide #407	$12.95		
Parenting: Ward & June ... #486	$12.95		
Peak Performance #469	$12.95		
The Polished Professional #426	$12.95		
The Power of Innovative Thinking #428	$12.95		
Powerful Leadership Skills for Women #463	$12.95		
Powerful Presentation Skills #461	$12.95		
Real Men Don't Vacuum #416	$12.95		
Self-Esteem: The Power to Be Your Best #4642	$12.95		
SELF Profile #403	$12.95		
The Stress Management Handbook #4842	$12.95		
Supreme Teams: How to Make Teams Work #4303	$12.95		
The Supervisor's Handbook #410	$12.95		
Team-Building #494	$12.95		
Techniques to Improve Your Writing Skills #460	$12.95		
The Windows Handbook #4303	$12.95		
The Write Stuff #414	$12.95		

Sales Tax
All purchases subject to state and local sales tax.
Questions?
Call
1-800-258-7248

Subtotal	$
Add 7% Sales Tax *(Or add appropriate state and local tax)*	$
Shipping and Handling *($1 one item; 50¢ each additional item)*	$
Total	$

VIP No. 705-008438-096

Buy 3 get 1 FREE!

60-MINUTE TRAINING SERIES™ HANDBOOKS

TITLE	RETAIL PRICE	QTY.	TOTAL
8 Steps for Highly Effective Negotiations #424	$12.95		
Assertiveness #442	$12.95		
Balancing Career and Family #415	$12.95		
Change: Coping with Tomorrow Today #421	$12.95		
Customer Service: The Key ... Customers #488	$12.95		
Dynamic Communication Skills for Women #413	$12.95		
Empowering the Self-Directed Team #422	$12.95		
Getting Things Done #411	$12.95		
How to Conduct Win-Win Perf. Appraisals #423	$12.95		
How to Find Your Way Around the Internet #4305	$12.95		
How to Manage Conflict #495	$12.95		
How to Manage Your Boss #493	$12.95		
Listen Up: Hear What's Really Being Said #4172	$12.95		
Managing Our Differences #412	$12.95		
Master Microsoft® Word #406	$12.95		
Motivation and Goal-Setting #4962	$12.95		
A New Attitude #4432	$12.95		
PC Survival Guide #407	$12.95		
Parenting: Ward & June ... #486	$12.95		
Peak Performance #469	$12.95		
The Polished Professional #426	$12.95		
The Power of Innovative Thinking #428	$12.95		
Powerful Leadership Skills for Women #463	$12.95		
Powerful Presentation Skills #461	$12.95		
Real Men Don't Vacuum #416	$12.95		
Self-Esteem: The Power to Be Your Best #4642	$12.95		
SELF Profile #403	$12.95		
The Stress Management Handbook #4842	$12.95		
Supreme Teams: How to Make Teams Work #4303	$12.95		
The Supervisor's Handbook #410	$12.95		
Team-Building #494	$12.95		
Techniques to Improve Your Writing Skills #460	$12.95		
The Windows Handbook #4303	$12.95		
The Write Stuff #414	$12.95		

Sales Tax
All purchases subject to state and local sales tax.
Questions?
Call
1-800-258-7248

Subtotal	$
Add 7% Sales Tax *(Or add appropriate state and local tax)*	$
Shipping and Handling *($1 one item; 50¢ each additional item)*	$
Total	$

VIP No. 705-008438-096